• ICL Creative Bible Learning Series •

Everything You Want to Know About

Teaching Children

GRADES 1-6

Barbara Bolton
Charles T. Smith and
Wesley Haystead

Published by Regal Books
A Division of GL Publications
Ventura, California 93006
Printed in U.S.A.

Library of Congress Cataloging in publication data

Bolton, Barbara J.
    Everything you want to know about teaching children (grades 1-6).

    Includes bibliographies.
    1. Christian education of children. I. Smith, Charles T. II. Title.
BV1475.2.B634   1987   268'.432   87-29723
ISBN 0-8307-1271-2

2 3 4 5 6 7 8 9 10 / 91 90 89 88

Rights for publishing this book in other languages are contracted by
Gospel Literature International (GLINT) foundation. GLINT also pro-
vides technical help for the adaptation, translation, and publishing of
Bible study resources and books in scores of languages worldwide. For
further information, contact GLINT, Post Office Box 488, Rosemead,
California, 91770, U.S.A., or the publisher.

Contents

The Authors   4

Preface   5

PART 1 ■ CHILDREN AND TEACHERS   7

1. Ministering to Children   9
2. The Teacher: A Guide and Fellow Learner   13
3. Understanding Today's Child   23
4. Children: Needs and Age Level Characteristics   33
5. Leading a Child to Christ   55

PART 2 ■ THE DYNAMICS OF LEARNING   63

6. Children's Learning Styles   65
7. Five Steps to Dynamic Learning   73
8. Conditions for Dynamic Learning   79
9. Facilities for Children   87
10. Grading, Grouping and Growing   99
11. An Effective Teaching Schedule   107
12. Productive Lesson Planning   117
13. Who Makes It Happen?   129

**PART 3 ■ SKILLS AND TIPS
FOR BETTER TEACHING**   139

14. How to Make Bible Stories Come Alive   141
15. How to Use Bible Learning Activities   157

The Authors

Barbara J. Bolton earned a B.A. degree at Whittier College and an M.A. degree in elementary education at California State College, Los Angeles. Barbara's 20-year teaching career spans kindergarten through sixth grade. She is a specialist in the field of remedial reading. Barbara has worked with Sunday School children and teachers from babies through the sixth grade levels. Her writing experience includes the development of varied curriculum materials. She is the author of *How to Do Bible Learning Activities: (Grades 1-6) Book 1* and *Book 2*. For several years Barbara conducted International Center for Learning Seminars and Clinics for children's teachers and leaders. She is currently Director of Children's Ministries at the Evangelical Free Church in Fullerton, California.

Charles T. Smith graduated with a B.A. degree from Western Baptist Bible College and with a M.R.E. degree (cum laude) from Talbot Theological Seminary. He has served four churches in California and one in Texas as a Director of Christian Education. Presently he is serving as Minister of Education at College Avenue Baptist Church in San Diego. For several years, Charles was an instructor in the Children's Division of the International Center for Learning.

Wesley Haystead is a Christian Education specialist. He received his Master's degree in educational psychology from the University of Southern California and has been working with children, teaching about them, and writing for them for more than 15 years. Currently, Wesley is Editorial Director at Lowell Brown Enterprises. He is the father of three children. He and his wife, Sheryl, live in Ventura, California.

Preface

The International Center for Learning is committed to obeying Christ's command to "go and make disciples . . . teaching them" (Matt. 28:19,20). To fulfill this great commission, ICL provides in-depth training resources for leaders ministering in churches of all sizes. ICL helps teachers discover how to motivate students to be involved in learning the life-changing truths of God's word.

This book is designed for both the new teacher and those who are more experienced. Barbara Bolton, Charles Smith and Wesley Haystead concisely present the needs and characteristics of children. They will help you discover a variety of ways you can provide effective Bible learning. These insights into your learners and the learning process will enable you to make the Bible come alive for your learners.

You can profit from reading this book alone and discussing it with a group of teachers. You will want to refer to this book many times for assistance in planning new methods and programs as well as improving what you are already doing.

PART 1

Children and Teachers

Ministering to Children

Why should helping children learn Bible truths fill you with excitement and enthusiasm? First, the biblical message is crucial to the life of each child. Second, your students are at the most reachable and teachable stage of their lives. While teaching a student subjects such as math or history is an important and meaningful task, the consequences of understanding such information is limited. However, guiding a child into a consciousness of the Lord Jesus equips him or her with the resources for dealing with all facets of life! What could be more essential!

YOUR MESSAGE

The central vitality of the Bible is its life-changing power. Not only do disillusioned adults need that message. Children, too, need to know of God's unconditional love that offers forgiveness for the past and help with the present and future. God's Word is "good news" to everyone—including children.

The first way to help your students know of the Bible's life-changing truth is to live it before them. This does not mean you must be a "spiritual giant." Start where you are. Begin honestly, opening your life to God's direction. As you prepare each lesson, ask yourself:

■ What difference does this Bible truth make in my own life?

■ What must I do to incorporate that Scripture into my everyday experience?

■ What shall I share from my own spiritual life that will help clarify those biblical truths to my students?

Every time you get ready to teach, ask the Lord to guide you in answering these three crucial questions.

Once you begin to deal personally with the dynamic message of the Bible, you'll see God move through your life; and you'll radiate the presence of Christ. As God's Spirit is freed to bring about change in your attitudes and actions, you'll find that your approach to teaching will come alive with deep meaning. Paul wrote, "Continue to work out your salvation with fear and trembling, for it is God who works in you to will and to act according to his good purpose" (Phil. 2:12,13). More and more you will be convinced that God can use you to help open young hearts and minds to Him and to His Word.

As you are consistently made aware that God is involved in people's lives, you will find it easy to present Bible learning experiences with genuine enthusiasm. You'll be excited that Bible truth has incredible, up-to-the-minute implications for children, that God's power is available to Christians today!

YOUR STUDENTS

Not only do you have a crucial message, but you are sharing it at a critical time, for your students are in the process of building their value system. An eight-year-old is already making spiritual and social decisions, and may be sensing a very real need for a relationship with God. Already that youngster may be facing conflicts between the Bible's teachings and the values of friends, as well as those of influential personalities in television, sports and books.

It's important for a child early in life to build a relationship with the Lord Jesus. Paul said of Timothy, "from infancy you have known the holy Scriptures, which are able to make you wise for salvation through faith in Christ Jesus" (2 Tim. 3:15). Children need to know Jesus' love and guidance are available now. A child may come to your class with an aching need: perhaps a family quarrel or difficulty; he may be doing poorly in school; a best friend may have moved. Unfortunately, the immediate response of that child who has the greatest need for Jesus' love may be quite negative. This high-need child may be disruptive, withdrawn or appear bored. Even when the child resists, however, the one thing that almost always communicates is your unconditional love.

The Lord Jesus demonstrated the need for love in guiding children that day He drew them into His arms. (see Mark 10:14-16.) Certainly those children must have been more touched by their precious moments with Jesus than by any number of sermons on the love of God. A child urgently needs to see biblical truths and values shown in the attitudes and actions of teachers, especially if such examples are not part of the child's life at home. Timothy was fortunate, for his family was the place where he first experienced the faith. "I have been reminded of your sincere faith, which first lived in your grandmother Lois and in your mother Eunice" (2 Tim. 1:5).

This kind of teaching and demonstration of love involves more than mere sentiment—it means commitment. Ministering effectively to the children in your class requires setting aside adequate time for your lesson preparation. Not to memorize a "canned" delivery, but to be familiar and comfortable with the material so that you're free to listen for clues from your students. A teacher who is perceptive can often sense a child's need for love and attention—and perhaps a special opportunity to lead that child into a relationship with the Lord Jesus.

Showing love to your students will certainly take more than an hour on Sunday morning. It requires time in prayer, on the phone, writing notes, attending baseball games or school programs or visiting homes; it may mean real sacrifice of your time and energy.

Paul carried such a person-centered, whole-life ministry to his converts. He describes his 24-hour workday among the Thessalonians as encompassing both the "caring mother" and "encouraging father" roles (see 1 Thess. 2:7,11). Then believers were so loved by Paul that they became his "glory and joy" (1 Thess. 2:20). You have unparalleled opportunity to present the Lord Jesus to your students at a crucial time in their lives.

The Teacher: A Guide and Fellow Learner

Let's talk about you, the one who guides children. You may be called a leader, teacher, assistant or helper. Whatever your title, you have a part in expressing God's love to a child. The church of Jesus Christ has entrusted you to help children know Him, love Him and serve Him. In accepting this responsibility, you have been called as surely as Moses was called that day at the burning bush—though possibly not as dramatically.

If you have ever doubted your qualifications to guide children, you are not alone. When Moses heard God's call, his response was, "I'm not the person for a job like that! . . . [The people] won't believe me! . . . I'm just not a good speaker" (Exod. 3:11; 4:1,10,*TLB*).

WHAT CHARACTERISTICS SHOULD A TEACHER POSSESS?

Growing

Peter exhorts us to "grow in the grace and knowledge of our Lord and Savior Jesus Christ" (2 Pet. 3:18). Continuing growth in all areas of Christian life is of primary importance for everyone who guides children. This growth comes by regularly attending church services, studying God's Word and fellowshipping with other Christians. The community of faith (fellowship of believers) is an essential part of the "support system" for a Christian.

Systematically, study key books of the Bible (either in a Bible study class or alone) to acquire a basic understanding of God's

Word and its teachings. Although you may not use all the information directly in your work with children, consistent Bible study will enrich your life and provide a resource on which to draw in specific situations. When your spiritual life is growing, you will be increasingly responsive to God's love and to the leading of the Holy Spirit.

Prayer must be a regular, meaningful part of your life. Paul wrote, "Do not be anxious about anything, but in everything, by prayer and petition, with thanksgiving, present your requests to God" (Phil. 4:6). Pray for each staff member in your department as well as for your own personal needs. Pray by name for each child in your class. Know each child's needs so your prayers can be specific. Pray for guidance in your lesson preparation; ask the Lord to help you make your teaching relevant as well as interesting to children.

In addition to growing spiritually, a teacher of children needs to be growing in understanding of child-level needs and interests. Children are a vital information source! If a teacher stops learning from children, children will soon stop learning from the teacher.

Teachable

"The intelligent man is always open to new ideas. In fact, he looks for them," wrote Solomon (Prov. 18:15, *TLB*). Those who guide children must be teachable. When you sense your high calling from God, you will want to fulfill your commitment in the best possible way. Be willing to learn new and better ways to do your job. Be open to new approaches suggested in your curriculum. Interact with others who teach children. Ask parents for ideas of activities their children enjoy. Attend workshops dealing with helping children learn.

Flexible

Anyone who guides children must be able to change according to the situation and interests of the children. At one moment you may be a question-answerer. At another moment a comforter, an arbitrator, a setter of limits or a storyteller. At times, you might be filling two or three roles simultaneously.

Caring

The one who guides children is a person who cares. The reality of Christ in your own life makes you care enough to want to share Him with others. You become excited when you see a child discover an evidence of God's love or show loving concern for another in response to God's Word.

Express your concern by loving and accepting each child just as he or she is. Often we reserve our concern for times of distress and trouble. Genuine love reaches out into all situations, the pleasant as well as the unpleasant. Understand the individual differences in children; become aware of the needs and potential of each child. Share the child's feeling of wonder and discovery. Enjoy a child's achievements, jokes and enthusiasm.

Because you care, always present a neat, well-groomed personal appearance. Use a soft, pleasing voice and have a ready smile.

A Guide

You also serve children as a guide. To some it might seem much easier to simply tell children all we think they should know. However, children learn far more through firsthand experiences than they do from sit-still-and-listen situations. Your role is to guide children in Bible learning experiences through which they can discover, create and accomplish meaningful things for themselves. Pattern your teaching ministry after the ultimate teacher, the Holy Spirit, who "will guide you into all truth" (John 16:13).

The direction in which you guide children's learning experiences is of utmost importance. Pay close attention to learning aims stated in your teacher's manual. A clear focus of where each lesson is headed will enable you to direct thoughts, conversations and activities toward a specific objective. Look for the ways the experiences suggested in each lesson help accomplish that lesson aim. Study the lesson material; thoroughly prepare for the parts of the schedule which you are to lead.

A Listener

Those who guide children are listeners. James advises us, "Everyone should be quick to listen, slow to speak" (Jas. 1:19). A child's words and actions are clues to needs and understanding. Watch facial expressions and body language. Listen carefully to a child's words. Avoid letting your mind race ahead to what you want to say next. Rather, use "active listening"—responding to a child by rephrasing his comments. For example, when Eric says, "I'm glad every day when reading time is over at my school!" you could say, "It sounds to me like you are really happy to be through reading."

By careful listening, an alert teacher can determine what concepts need clarifying and which aims need reinforcing. Most important, your careful and thoughtful listening encourages a child to communicate with you.

Enthusiastic

Enthusiasm is also an essential ingredient of those who teach children. To excite others about learning God's Word, a teacher needs to be genuinely enthusiastic. Be sure your feelings are real! How quickly children spot hypocrisy!

WHAT ARE A TEACHER'S RESPONSIBILITIES?

Think back to the teacher who meant the most in your life. The one you remember most clearly no doubt loved you and showed concern for you. This memorable teacher recognized you as a valued individual, understood your needs and attempted to satisfy them. This teacher may have been firm with you, not allowing you to be satisfied with a mediocre performance. Your self-esteem increased as you felt secure in the concern and love of this effective teacher.

Let's think about specific ways you can enable your students to experience the reality of God's love in their own lives.

Build Relationships

The unconditional kind of love the Lord Jesus demonstrated in His ministry should be basic in each encounter you have with children. Your minutes together can be some of the best ones of the entire week, both for the children and for you.

These productive times together begin as you build an accepting and warm relationship with each child in your class. Such relationships serve as foundation stones in Christian nurture. Begin this kind of relationship by accepting each child "as is." Commit yourself to love Brian just the way he is now and not for what you hope he may become. Take time to find out the things Amanda enjoys or dislikes. Listen attentively to Joey as he talks to you. Recognize and respect Janine's feelings. Show understanding for Sean's point of view. Encourage Ashley's efforts and recognize her successes! Be ready with expressions of genuine praise and encouragement.

Another important aspect in building relationships is to help each child learn to know you well; only then will a child feel a bond with you and thus desire to take on your Christlike characteristics. Paul wrote to the Corinthians, "Follow my example, as I follow the example of Christ" (1 Cor. 11:1). You need to be transparent to the child in order to aid this identification process (the unconscious acquiring of characteristics, beliefs, values). Share your own relationship with Christ, being honest about times of failure and emphasizing evidence of growth.

Also, help the children to know and appreciate each other even though Sunday may be the only time during the week they see one another. Working together in learning activities will lead them to experience how the Body of Christ functions—together as a team, not in competition, but in harmony.

Provide Choices

Plan for children to have a choice of appropriate, aim-related activities in which they can participate. When you offer a choice, you are recognizing that all children are not alike, that they possess differing interests, skills and abilities. The choice is not whether a child participates or does nothing, but rather an option of which activity he or she prefers in order to learn. You may allow a child to decide whether to write or draw an answer to a question, whether to work alone or with a friend, whether to read instructions or listen to them on a prepared audiotape. You may also offer a choice among two or more activities. For example, a child may decide if he or she wants to help make a rebus song chart or prepare puppets for a dramatization. Both of these activities will help accomplish a specific Bible learning aim.

Stimulate Learning

Providing an environment which stimulates learning is another teacher responsibility. Begin by keeping your room clean and attractive. Avoid clutter! Arrange materials so they are seeable, reachable and returnable. Use bulletin board space to display some of the children's Bible Learning Activities or similar work. Keep seasonal pictures and displays current. Easter pictures still posted in July tell all those who enter the room, "No one cares."

A child's learning is also stimulated as you provide a variety of learning activities. Firsthand experiences encourage a child to think and reason. The thrill of discovery is an exhilarating experience. What better way for children to become excited about learning God's Word!

Recognize Positive Behavior

During the time you are with a child, focus on positive behavior. When Jesus met Zacchaeus, Jesus did not immediately tell Zacchaeus all the bad things that He knew about him. Rather, Jesus began by building a friendly relationship with Zacchaeus. Jesus affirmed Zacchaeus by calling his name and by being friendly with him. For a publican to be treated with such favor was overwhelming. Zacchaeus's beliefs and behavior were revolutionized through this encounter (see Luke 19).

Frequently a teacher feels the necessity to point out to children the things they do wrong. Rather, dwell on those things they do right! Affirm children, rather than illuminate the negative aspect of their actions. For example, be alert to a child's acceptable behavior. Then comment (either privately or in the group), "Darrin, I really liked the way you helped Kevin read those words he didn't know. That's a good way to be a kind friend!" Be specific! The child needs to know exactly what merited your praise because very likely the child will want to repeat the behavior. "You're a good kid" gives no clue.

Be sure each child in your class hears at least one specific and honest compliment from you sometime during each session. The apostle Paul reminds us, "If you love someone you will be loyal to him no matter what the cost. You will always believe in him, always expect the best of him, and always stand your ground in defending him" (1 Cor. 13:7, *TLB*).

Have Realistic Expectations

Teachers need to be realistic and consistent in what they expect of children. For example, recognize that a first grader cannot sit still for extended periods of time. A growing body demands action! Understand the age characteristics of the children you teach (see chapter 4). Are they in a spurt of physical growth? What is their energy level? How do they relate to their peers? How do they express their emotions?

Being aware of an individual child's characteristics is also an important part of your teaching responsibility. For example, some children work at a faster pace than others; some take pride in neat work, while others are content with a slap-dash effort. Some children have very creative ideas, while others respond in rather traditional ways. As you guide children, keep in mind each child's individual strengths and weaknesses. Encourage each child to work in the way that meets his or her needs. Avoid comparing children's work.

Reach Beyond the Classroom

A major study of educational research and practice came to the conclusion that time is the single most important ingredient in the impact of a teacher on a student. "Given a particular student and a particular teacher, the *length of time they are together* influences student learning more than anything else."[1]

It is important for the Sunday School leader or teacher to plan additional contact with each student beyond that which occurs at church on Sunday morning. The child's home and neighborhood are obvious places to gain information and understanding of each child. When you visit, find out if your student is the youngest, oldest or the middle child in the family. Discover the kinds of school experiences that are part of the child's life. Learn about special interests and how they may be related to spiritual, emotional, social, intellectual and physical growth.

Plan for outings with a small group of children so that each may have an extra share of your love and interest. A visit to your home by a few students at a time fosters a closer relationship with you and with each other. It gives your students the opportunity to observe you in an informal setting and see how your actions and your attitude are patterned after those of Christ.

As you become better acquainted with your students, you will discover additional and practical ways to minister to their needs. Think about including one or two of the following ideas in your schedule this week:

Ministry is . . .

■ Taking a child to a doctor's appointment for a working mother.

■ Child-sitting while parents house hunt.

■ Sitting with a sick baby while mother takes a breather and goes grocery shopping.

■ Praising a child for the way he handles his crutches.

■ Giving a birthday party for a child of migrant workers and keeping in touch by letters when the family has moved on.

■ Making special efforts to attend the music recitals, school plays or athletic events of the children in your class.

■ Cultivating friendships with children who seem to have no particular problems.

■ Helping a child face the death of a loved one. Allow

moments of tender sadness and use conversation to prevent development of misconceptions because adults in his family are caught in periods of depression.

Lead Children in Ministry to Others

A significant part of your teaching responsibility involves helping children minister to others (according to a child's age level, capabilities and spiritual development). When you have a unit of lessons dealing with love or kindness, assist children in thinking of practical and realistic ways to help people. Children will enjoy the opportunity of going with you to visit another child or a shut-in. Guide children to make cookies or a cheery greeting card as a gift to take along. They will respond eagerly to your friendly guidance. Remind children of Hebrews 13:16, "And do not forget to do good and to share with others." Check your curriculum for ideas appropriate to your learners' abilities and interests.

NOTE

1. Henry M. Brickell, "How to Change What Matters," *Educational Leadership*, (December, 1980), p. 202.

Understanding Today's Child

In many respects children are the same from one generation to the next. There are some things, however, that distinguish the children of today from those of previous years. We often view children in terms of our own childhood or our own immediate Christian family situation. However, our society is changing drastically from one generation to the next, producing conditions and consequences of which many adults may not be aware. A combination of the following circumstances describes much of the world of children today.

THE FAMILY

Today's family is shrinking. This depopulation is not only due to the declining birth rate, but also to divorce. The rate of divorce has more than doubled since 1960, as has the number of children involved in the dissolution of their parent's marriage. In 1960, 463,000 children had experienced the divorce of their parents. Just two decades later, the number increased to 1,180,000![1]

One of the most devastating results of divorce involving children is the loss of companionship and even contact from the noncustodial parent. Over half of the children of divorce who do not live with their father do not see him even once a year![2]

When a school-age child's parents are divorced, fears and anxiety often give way to feelings of anger, frustration, guilt, resentment, hopelessness or rejection. The school years generally thought of as a person's most carefree and happy times, become loaded with depression. Rather than being free to explore interests and enjoy learning, the child is caught in a web of insecurities.

Single-parent families, which may result from death and illegitimacy as well as separation and divorce, are becoming increasingly common. One fourth of all school-aged children now live in a single-parent home, and over the course of this decade, half of all children under 10 will have spent time in a single-parent home.[3] At least one out of every eight women giving birth are unmarried[4] and more than four times as many children were born to an unwed mother in 1980 as in 1950.[5]

The difficulties faced by the North American family are also due to the fact that, for the first time in our national history, most children now have mothers who work outside the home and most of these mothers work full time.[6] More than half of all school-age children in two-parent families have mothers who are employed outside the home.[7] Economic pressures and the desire to find greater individual fulfillment seem to be the prime reasons for mothers' employment.

These changes have had significant impact on the makeup of the "typical" family. Just since 1970, there has been nearly a 10 percent decrease in the percentage of families with children in which a married couple is present. More than 20 percent of all families with children are now single-parent homes.[8]

Still another reason for change in the makeup of a family is the growing disappearance of non-parental relatives from families. The numbers of grandparents, aunts and uncles found in both single- and two-parent families has dropped significantly in the past generation.

The mobility of all families frequently takes children out of any kind of sustained contact and relationship with blood relatives. The lack of intergenerational activity, apart from that between parent and child, has the tendency to sever the natural transference of accumulated experiences and knowledge of one generation to another. The number of families moving to a new home has declined slightly in recent years, but about 16 percent of families still change residences in any given year.[9]

One evidence of severe family trouble is parental neglect or abuse of a child. While relatively few families are touched by this trauma, the rate of such cases, which remained fairly stable until 1970, increased by 50 percent through 1980.[10]

Whether this increase is due to worsening conditions for many children or simply greater awareness of the problem by official agencies, everyone who works with children must be aware of the possibility of encountering a traumatic situation.

Another alarming and growing indicator of the stress all these factors create is child suicide, which has increased dramatically since 1970.[11] Obviously the child is trying to call attention to a very desperate situation. An important signal of suicide is depression, an ailment psychiatry did not even recognize in children until the 1960s.[12]

Perhaps the figures on child suicides are so disturbing because the 10-year period from age 5 through 14 has long been, and continues to be, the safest and healthiest time of life. The death rate for this period is always less than half that of any other 10-year span, and is also less than half that of the first five years.[13]

A growing number of children do not experience childhood as an idyllic time of loving and protected nurture. This discovery is very unsettling to our view of childhood in today's world.

COMMUNICATION

Our culture is one of electronic communication—computer, video, compact discs, transistor radios, television, audiotapes, movies and pictures in newspapers. World happenings are rapidly communicated to our children so that they live in the middle of history-making events. Years ago, the child's world included only community and occasional national events. Now the entire world parades before him!

Ninety-nine percent of American homes contain TVs and elementary aged children average four to five hours of television watching a day![14]

The importance of money, beauty, intelligence and brawn are all too often glorified on the screen. These become the channels through which people must attain worth. Inferiority feelings inevitably develop when children sense, however inaccurately, that they do not measure up to the direct and subliminal standards of the media.

Coping with inferiority has become the unconscious obsession of millions of children. The total effect of the media upon a child's self-concept is underlined by a theologian, "The media culture becomes a kind of touchstone for one's own perceptions .... People begin to distrust their own ideas and impulses if they are not corroborated by the media. The signals begin to prescribe not only what is good and true, but what is real."[15]

MOBILITY

Typically 35 million Americans move every year, 22 million within the same county. The children who are caught in the family moves have less chance to establish roots in a community before moving again. Stability of family life is affected. Close human and community relationships have little time to develop under such circumstances, whether in school, church or neighborhood. Insecurity may develop within a child who does not make new friends easily.

A significant number of people in our society have demonstrated the ultimate in mobility: they have immigrated from other countries. The number of immigrants, legal and illegal, has increased dramatically in the last decade, creating the likelihood that your community contains children who were born in another culture, or whose parents were born there.[16]

VALUES

Today's children are living in a culture that no longer supports the Christian code of morality held by our nation from the time of its founding. Moral decay and corruption in all realms of society are some things that are accepted by many as a matter of fact.

Children today are being raised in a society that glamorizes premarital and extramarital sex, condones homosexuality and abortion, makes divorce easy, stimulates drug abuse and permits pornographic magazines and films to exist—even those that exploit children!

Futhermore, the moral climate of today's culture recognizes no absolutes—no real "rights" or "wrongs." Everything, seemingly, is relative (dependent on the situation, not on moral law). This moral confusion is further compounded when there exists an empty or weak spiritual nature on the part of parents, making them incapable of defensive or offensive action.

Many people have found positive signs that another dimension of our moral climate seems to be slowly emerging. Various surveys in the past decade have indicated that America is experiencing a religious revival. Some polls have shown that church attendance is on an upturn, and more Americans believe religious influence is increasing in recent years. Other polls have shown an increase in interest in religion in general.

However, while people may claim to be more "religious" than before, Sunday School attendance statistics show significant declines in recent years. Total Sunday School enrollment in America declined by 24 percent between 1970 and 1980, with the decline occurring in both mainline and evangelical churches. Even the few denominations that have shown Sunday School enrollment growth, have not seen their Sunday Schools keep up with general church membership.[17]

In addition, the actual number of adults attending church has continued to decline. In 1960, 49 percent of adults claimed to have attended church within the past seven days of being questioned. By 1970 the number had dropped to 42 percent. And by 1980, the number dropped again to just 40 percent. Even more disturbing is that the decline was greatest in the 18-30 age group—those who are or soon will be parents of the children we teach![18]

This pattern tells us that reaching and winning unchurched children and their families needs to be a top priority of every Sunday School leader and teacher.

DRUGS AND DELINQUENCY

A generation ago, drugs were considered a problem for only a small percentage of lower-class youth and adults. In the '60s and '70s, drugs exploded through the youth culture, and today are a growing menace at the elementary school level. Dealing with so-called "recreational" drugs in a community is often made difficult because of today's parents being the first generation that widely experimented with drugs themselves.

Often related to drug abuse is a growing problem of delinquency involving younger children in more serious crimes. Delinquency cases (excluding traffic violations) in Juvenile Courts nearly tripled between 1960 and 1980.[19]

In every group of children today, there is likely to be at least one who is on the way toward serious drug and/or delinquency problems unless some caring adult intervenes to help break the pattern of rebellion and distrust.

ANTI-CHILDISHNESS

Part of the frustration children experience today results from parents urging their children to "grow up." These insistent parents are concerned primarily with what their children will someday become—adults—rather than what they are now—children.

The noisiness and nonsense of childhood are disliked. So children soon discover that when they display adultlike behavior, they are accepted and rewarded. Teachers, too, want children to sit down and be quiet, to produce, to conform, to be mini-adults.

Adultlike pressures insist that children excel in everything; they must match the achievements of other children, adjust as well socially as do their peers, and possess a high I.Q.

Thus an enormous burden is placed upon children as society pushes them to face issues beyond their developmental level, situations too complex for their comprehension, and expectations too unrealistic for them to attain. The result of too much pressure is a child beset by chronic anxiety. Intensely competitive, driven behavior marks some of these children, while others become lethargic or suffer tension headaches and high blood pressure.[20]

We must recognize that every stage of childhood is vital to ultimate psychological, physical, intellectual and social well-being. It is crucial that those involved in ministry to children expect children to think, act and respond like children and not like miniature adults.

EDUCATIONAL CHANGES

Dramatic changes have been occurring in elementary school education. The public school system has come under extensive fire for many perceived and actual shortcomings: overcrowding, busing, secularism, poor performance, violence, etc. The National Commission on Excellence in Education published a dramatic report, asserting that the public schools were threatened by a "rising tide of mediocrity."[21] While many educators and leaders have debated their findings and recommendations, this report, and many others, are evidence of deep concern and often disagreements over the way in which children are being taught.

The turmoil in public school education has led many parents to move their children into private schools. Recent years have also seen a growing movement toward home schools, especially on the part of Christian parents who find the public schools operate in opposition to many Christian values.

Regardless of the current state of secular education, Christian teachers need to remember that for a child to develop to his or her God-given potential, the Sunday School must be geared to help meet individual needs. There should be a healthy balance between a child's knowing Bible information, understanding its relevance and translating that knowledge into behavior. The Christian teacher must be committed to developing a positive, accepting relationship with students and simultaneously guiding those students in the study and appropriation of relevant Bible content.

NOTES

1. *Statistical Abstract of the United States: 1985, 105th Edition* (Washington DC: United States Department of Commerce, 1984), p. 80.
2. Lenore J. Weitzman, *The Divorce Revolution,* (New York: The Free Press, 1985).
3. Leroy E. Hay, "New World, New Kids, New Basics," *The Great School Debate,* Beatrice and Ronald Gross, Editors, (New York: Simon and Schuster, 1985), p. 219.
4. *Statistical Abstract,* p. 64.
5. *Ibid,* p. 46.
6. *Ibid,* p. 62.
7. *Ibid,* p. 57.
8. *Ibid,* p. 80.
9. *Ibid,* p. 16.
10. *Ibid,* p. 182.
11. "Children's Suicide Rate Shows Big Increase," *San Diego Union,* (December 12, 1976), p. A-14.
12. Kenneth Kenniston, "Do Americans Really Like Children?" *Childhood Education,* Vol. 52, No. 1, (October 1975), p. 7.
13. *Statistical Abstract,* p. 71.
14. Dorothy Singer, "Reading, Imagination, and Television," *School Library Journal, Volume 26,* (December 1979), pp. 31-34.
15. Kenneth Curtis, "Telecult," *Eternity,* (November 1976), p. 14.

16. *Statistical Abstract*, p. 85.
17. Charles Arn, Donald McGavran and Win Arn, *Growth: A New Vision for the Sunday School* (Pasadena, CA: Church Growth Press, 1980), pp. 29-34.
18. *Statistical Abstract*, p. 52.
19. Ibid., p. 182.
20. David Elkind, *The Hurried Child* (Reading, MA: Addison-Wesley, 1981), pp. 165-182.
21. National Commission on Excellence in Education, *A Nation at Risk* (Washington, DC: U.S. Government Printing Office, 1983).

Children: Needs and Age Level Characteristics

God has entrusted teachers of children in the church with opportunities to help them learn vital scriptural truths. An effective teacher is aware of children's needs, how children grow and develop; also how these processes influence children's attitudes and actions—particularly as related to ways they learn best.

THEIR NEEDS

As we consider the growth and development pattern of children, we look at those patterns in terms of individual children. For the Lord made each child different from all others. However, regardless of where a child is in the ebb and flow of growth, every child shares certain basic needs, needs that have a direct bearing on success or failure in the learning process.

Love, Acceptance and Security

A child develops a sense of value and worth—healthy self-esteem—through experiencing love and acceptance from parents, teachers and peers. The secure feeling of being loved is the foundation on which a child can build love toward others. The child learns to love by being loved. How clearly the Lord originally demonstrated this principle to us! "We love because he first loved us" (1 John 4:19).

Every child needs generous measures of acceptance, feeling unconditionally accepted as is, regardless of behavior or appearance. If a child is made to feel he or she must earn acceptance, feelings of insecurity and unworthiness may result. Rebellious or aggressive behavior may be the way of attracting attention and reflecting the need to be loved and accepted.

Scripture rings loud and clear with God's unconditional acceptance of us. The Bible teaches that none of us can ever do anything or ever be good enough to earn His acceptance and love. "But God demonstrates his own love for us in this: While we were still sinners, Christ died for us" (Rom. 5:8). Those words describe God's incredible acceptance of us!

The child who feels loved and accepted by adults finds it easy to feel accepted by God. Every teacher of Bible truth should avoid giving a child any impression that God will not love a child who behaves badly. God's love is a free, unconditional gift. God never withholds love to secure obedience. God loves so fully and faithfully that obedience to Him becomes the response of those who accept His amazing love and grace.

While we may not always approve of a child's behavior, we can always accept that child as a worthwhile person. Approval and acceptance are two different concepts. Acceptance means recognizing another person's feelings without judging or condemning. Acceptance does not mean permitting that person to demonstrate unacceptable behavior.

To accept a child means understanding a child. A wise teacher observes each child thoughtfully. Arrange a visit to the home of each one. Listen to the child's chatter. Talk and work with each child on an individual basis. Understanding provides a sound basis for accepting and loving.

As a child moves through these years of middle childhood, life's horizons continually widen to encompass experiences and people beyond home and family. The approval of adults in a child's life forms a base for growing feelings of security. While a child will periodically seek to act independently of adult authority, there is always a deep-seated need for approval—or even disapproval—from teachers and parents. To be noticed by an adult is of high value to a child.

The approval of a child's age-mates is referred to as "peer approval." The need for this approval is part of a child's deep-seated desire to belong—to be accepted by the group. In the

Sunday School setting, plan ways for children to make individual contributions in particular activities that will result both in their feeling accepted and in their acceptance of others.

The teacher is responsible to see that this approval need is met on a continuing basis. The children who most need approval often present the greatest challenge to the teacher. Make a special effort to provide opportunities for these children to succeed and be recognized. Church experiences for all children should be success-oriented. No child should need to struggle to the point of frustration in a skill or knowledge area.

Self-esteem is one pathway by which a child can develop a successful identity. When a child feels that he or she can make worthwhile contributions, and is aware of possessing abilities that can be used with positive results, that child will likely develop the healthy self-image and sense of personal worth so necessary to personal success.

Never underestimate the importance of love, acceptance and security in the learning process.

Choices and Challenges

A child learns to assume responsibility by being given the opportunity to make choices. Children who are never allowed to make choices or to experience different ways of learning have difficulty in adjusting when they are presented with a new situation.

Children are designed to learn in a variety of ways. Some of this potential goes unused because teachers make no provision for new experiences. All too often teachers become so comfortable with a method or a procedure that learners can predict with accuracy just what will happen next and how it will happen. No wonder children are bored!

Allowing a child the opportunity to make choices increases motivation, which results in better learning. For example, offer more than one Bible Readiness experience and Bible Learning Activity from which children may choose (see chapter 11). Also offer options of how an activity may be completed. For example, you may suggest children can complete a Bible verse puzzle using their open Bibles, or, to make the puzzle more difficult they may choose to keep their Bibles closed.

As you plan learning experiences, be sure to include activities that require different skills. Such a procedure recognizes the individual differences in children as well as their varying abilities in learning. For example, if every activity you offer involves reading and writing skills, then the child doesn't have much of a choice. Each week include experiences involving nonacademic skills (art, music, etc.) as well as academic ones. (See "Resources" sections in this book for sources of activity.)

Once you have offered a choice, be willing to accept the choice of the learner. To ensure that you can accept the child's decision, plan and phrase your choices so the alternatives are equally acceptable to you: "Would you rather work on the Bible verse puzzle or listen to a new song on the cassette player?" Avoid offering choices that invite children to suggest options you may not be able to follow: "What would you like to do next?" or "Does anyone have a favorite song?"

Consider the needs and interests of your students and incorporate activities to meet these needs. Allowing a child to make a choice says you feel he or she is capable and can be trusted. A boost to self-esteem!

Praise and Recognition

Every child needs to be recognized as a worthwhile individual. Teachers should focus on a child's positive behavior by deliberately looking for his strengths—the things the child does well. Criticism, ridicule and sarcasm only retard a child's development by tearing down self-image.

Praise for an honest attempt must be part of your relationship with children. Often teachers express praise only when the final goal is achieved; be sure to recognize the efforts of a child who tried, but did not complete the task. A sincere attempt, while resulting in partial completion, may deserve praise just as much as the finished task.

Praise must be genuine. How quickly children recognize our

insincerity! And praise must be specific. Avoid vague expressions that leave the child unsure of what was done well. Each Sunday be sure every child hears at least one honest compliment from you. "Keith, your handwriting gets more readable every week. Good work!" "Susan, I really appreciate your doing the extra cleanup chores today!" "Tom, you did a good job matching those words with the correct Bible reference. You really know how to do research!"

Sincere praise and recognition are important factors in the development of a child's self-esteem. A child's confidence is built up layer by layer. Continually pointing out weakness creates a feeling of inadequacy and unworthiness. But emphasizing good qualities builds inner strength.

Independence and Responsibility

Children need increased opportunities to gain personal independence in order to become a mature adult. The classroom should be organized so learners can accept the responsibility for care of materials. For example, consistently arrange equipment and supplies so children can locate, use and return materials as needed. Material carefully organized (well-labeled boxes, etc.) encourages children to accept responsibility for its use and care. Providing this kind of guidance also encourages children to be good stewards of the resources the Lord has entrusted to them.

Another way to guide children in accepting responsibility is by appointing helpers to be in charge of materials and classroom care. Rotate these jobs so all learners can participate. Establish and communicate routine cleanup and care procedures. Be sure children understand clearly what is expected of them. How often teachers have stayed to clean a work area when the learners should have cared for the cleanup as they completed their project.

The additional effort and patience required to allow learners to become increasingly independent and responsible for actions will prove valuable to teachers and learners alike. Not only will the children be given more opportunity to practice good patterns, but the teachers will also benefit in the growing process, since they will be looked upon as leaders, rather than "enforcers."

AGE LEVEL CHARACTERISTICS*

Each child is made in the image of God and yet no two are alike. Each child's interest and abilities are different from every other child's. Also, each child develops at a unique rate. This rate of growth is determined by many factors, including health and environment. Although each child moves at his or her own pace, each one passes through essentially the same growth pattern.

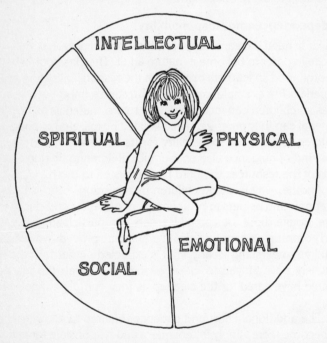

*Gospel Light has concise summaries of these age level characteristics available in 8½ × 11-inch pads for distribution to teachers and aides. Ask your supplier for *Age Level Characteristics (Grades 1-6)*.

Specific characteristics evident in this pattern of development make it possible to generally predict how a child will respond at a certain age. Keep these characteristics in mind as you plan Bible learning experiences appropriate for the child; but never let these general growth and development patterns become a mold into which you expect every child to fit at a specific age.

Although growth is continuous and orderly, it is uneven. Think of a child's development as a series of hills and valleys rather than a smooth, inclining plane.

Physical Growth

Six- and Seven-Year-Old Children ◼ After the rapid physical development of a childs's preschool years, the six- or seven-year-old is going through a period of slower growth. Great excitement accompanies the loss of each baby tooth! To the child it is an outward sign of growing up, a much anticipated experience for first and second graders.

The child's small muscle coordination is developing and improving so that handwriting is usually quite legible and cutting is becoming accurate. Girls are generally ahead of boys in small muscle development. Large muscle control allows a first and second grader increasing skill in playing ball and learning to master a bike. Each new physical achievement also brings additional status.

The term *constant motion* may be used to describe the behavior of sixes and sevens. With this storehouse of energy it is difficult for them to move slowly or to stay neat and clean. Sitting still for extended periods is physically difficult for most first and second graders.

As you plan learning experiences for your class, include opportunities for children to move about, as necessary. Frequent changes of pace (see schedule suggestions in chapter 11) must be built into your Sunday morning schedule to provide physical movement so necessary for growing bodies.

First and second graders are increasing in their ability to sing on pitch. With some guidance, they can sing rounds. Their improved muscle control allows most of them to clap rhythmic patterns successfully.

Eight- and Nine-Year-Old Children ■ Physically, the growth rate of an eight- and nine-year-old is steady but not spectacular. Both large and small muscle coordination is well enough developed to allow speed and accuracy in work and play. Girls continue to be ahead of boys in physical development, especially in small muscle control.

Children enjoy working hard to develop physical skills such as playing soccer, jumping rope and swimming. The seemingly endless repetition of bouncing and catching a ball makes little sense to an adult. But for the child, practice is necessary to perfect a skill. And with mastery of these skills comes approval from both peers and adults.

Eights and nines have an adequate supply of energy to work diligently for increased periods of time on projects of interest to them. Sometimes they become impatient at delay or inability to quickly accomplish desired goals. When a child's self-expectations become unrealistic, a sympathetic teacher should tactfully help rethink the plan into a more realistic one.

In planning for your class, take into account the independence these eight-and nine-year-olds have acquired. They no longer need the physical assistance of their earlier years. For example, after you have given clear and specific instructions, offer opportunities for these children to mix their own tempera paint or saw dowels. Also, children need the opportunity to assume almost all the responsibility for cleanup procedures.

Ten- and Eleven-Year-Old Children ■ The ten-year-old child is usually very healthy and full of energy. Large and small muscle control is well developed, enabling the child to participate successfully in many "doing" activities, such as assembling a complicated model. Mastery of physical skills gives a child a sense of personal satisfaction and a feeling of achievement.

Ten-year-old boys are usually willing to participate in activities involving both girls and boys although same-sex groupings are their dominant social form. Girls have not yet reached the growth spurt that will put them temporarily ahead of the boys in size. The ten-year-old is on a plateau before the period of adolescence.

Both the ten- and eleven-year-olds are active and curious. They are interested in the world about them. They deliberately seek a wide variety of new and different experiences.

Physical changes account for the fact that many eleven-year-olds tire easily. Some girls have begun the physical growth spurt and are taller than many boys of the same age. Eleven-year-old boys are often restless and wiggly. They need to be able to explore and investigate to find answers to questions and problems. During this year, boys more often work and play with boys, while girls seek out other girls.

As you plan your sessions, be aware the eleven-year-olds generally enjoy talking, listening and reading. However, unless these youngsters are sufficiently motivated, they find boring the repetition of skills they have fairly well perfected. For example, rather than asking a child (or several children) to read the information needed to complete a Bible Learning Activity, record the instructions on a cassette tape recorder. Also, consider creative ways (decoding, rebus, sand writing, Bible verse games) for child to memorize Bible verses. (See "Resources" sections for sources of creative activities.)

Emotional Growth

Another primary factor in a child's development is emotional growth. We can expect children to express feelings of anger, fear, jealousy and frustration. But we can also expect to see them radiate love, joy and wonder. Although we value these positive feelings, we need to remember that it is not the emotion, but rather the way it is expressed that determines whether it builds or damages a child's development.

Six- and Seven-Year-Old Children ■ Emotionally, the six- and seven-year-old is experimenting with new and frequently intense feelings. There is such a deep need for approval from both adults and peers that at times a child will exhibit unacceptable behavior to meet that need. How sad that a child must resort to such measures! Be sure each child in your class knows and feels your love. Express your affection by showing a genuine interest in the child and the child's interests and activities. Recognize each one's accomplishments.

Be especially aware of the child who seldom succeeds. Find ways for this child to experience success, no matter how inconsequential that experience may seem to you. Since children long to be recognized as individuals, names are important. Use a child's name frequently. Encourage class members to call one another (and you) by name.

Sometimes a first or second grader is unable to control his or her behavior. Anger or frustration is usually self-centered; the child often expresses these feelings physically.

These youngsters are emotionally bound to home, but at the same time enjoy adventuring out into a strange and sometimes confusing world. Although making decisions is difficult, it's important for a child to have a choice. Making a decision, then assuming the responsibility for that decision is vital to a child's development.

Seeking independence is a primary goal for this age although the child must often retreat to being dependent. Create opportunities for children to handle situations independently. For example, say, "Mark, we will soon be working in our *Student Guides*. I need you to help me get things we will need." The behavior of sixes and sevens is generally eager, enthusiastic and filled with the enjoyment of life.

Eight- and Nine-Year-Old Children ■ The emotional growth and development of eight- and nine-year-olds often surpasses their physical growth. They are curious and frequently attempt projects beyond their capabilities. For example, a child may eagerly begin making a complex puppet, only to discover his or her skills and interest span are inadequate for its completion.

This is the age of teasing, nicknames and criticism. These third and fourth graders use their increased verbal skills to vent their anger rather than resorting to the physical means of their younger years.

The eight-year-old is torn between the need to be a child and the desire to be grown up. The child is able to evaluate feelings and actions with peers, but finds it more difficult to accept constructive criticism from adults. Our eight-year-old is reaching out to others and becoming more concerned for other people than just for self. The child is developing a sense of fair play and is concerned with a value system that distinguishes between right and wrong.

The nine-year-old is more independent and skilled in making choices. Nines are increasingly aware of the larger world and are concerned with the rights and feelings of others beyond the family.

The nine-year-old is searching for self-identity. What a marvelous opportunity for teachers to provide a Christian model at a time when the child is eagerly searching for one!

Teachers need to provide the child with a variety of opportunities in which a sense of industry may thrive. These experiences should encourage creativity and enhance self-concept.

Ten- and Eleven-Year-Old Children ■ The ten-year-old has reached an emotional balance, and is a delight to the adults and friends. The ten is usually cooperative, easygoing, content, friendly and agreeable. Most adults enjoy working with this age group. The ten-year-old may evidence feelings of anger, but is quick to return to a happy personality. Even though both girls and boys begin to think about their future as adults, their interests tend to differ significantly.

We need to be aware of behavioral changes that result from the eleven-year-old's emotional growth. This child is experiencing unsteady emotions and often shifts from one mood to another. Peers' perceptions vitally affect the child's feelings, which move from sadness, dejection and anger, to happiness. We can frequently observe indications of jealousy or fear. Elevens are easily drawn to tears. All of these emotions are a part of the journey from childhood to adulthood. Changes of feelings require patient understanding from adults. And there is a strong need to be given opportunities to make choices and decisions with only the necessary limits that may be set by adults.

The eleven-year-old will work for long periods of time and with concentration and enthusiasm on projects that catch interest and have meaning. The child will often go far beyond the expectations set for him by adults. Alert teachers need to provide a choice of interesting and challenging learning experiences.

As the fifth and sixth graders mature, they continue to need a loving and accepting relationship with the significant adults in their lives. Although these youngsters don't rely on the more obvious ways of gaining attention and approval, they still want to share their problems and success with understanding adults.

Social Growth

Six- and Seven-Year-Old Children ■ The preschooler was interested in pleasing parents. In first and second grade the child is also concerned with pleasing teachers. Sixes and sevens struggle to become socially acceptable to their peer groups. The concept of "do to others what you would have them do to you" (Matt. 7:12) is a difficult one for these youngsters to accept. Being first and winning are still very important. Taking turns remains a difficult idea. A child needs opportunities to practice turn-taking in a variety of situations. Teachers need to help children accept the opinions and wishes of others, to enable the individual child to think about the welfare of the group.

A seven-year-old increases in concern for making friends and for peer approval. As you guide children, plan opportunities to help them develop the skills needed to plan and work in group situations. Be alert to give friendly guidance if a child has difficulty in accepting group decisions. Ask questions to help children resolve the situation. To enhance peer esteem, call attention to the achievements of several children who have cooperated successfully. For example, "I liked the puppet show this group gave us. They really know how to work well together!"

Both six- and seven-year-olds need the friendship of understanding adults. Children need help to value themselves as persons, and then to value each individual they know. A child's social growth process involves a movement from "I" to "you" to "we".

Eight- and Nine-Year-Old Children ■ Socially, the eight-year-old's interest is with the peer group. It is important to fit in and belong. As the desire to have status with friends becomes more intense, dependence upon adults decreases. At this time, the loving, understanding guidance of adults can be supportive as disagreements and problems occur with peers in group activities.

Even though the eight-year-old is working for group approval, it is important to have a special friend. This special relationship often develops with children of the same sex. Also, a child's activities and interests usually reflect those of the same sex.

Group influence continues to increase in the life of the nine-year-old. These youngsters can plan and implement a cooperative activity with real enthusiasm and success. It's an ideal time to emphasize church-related group activities or clubs into the Christian education program of the church.

The child's widening interest in people beyond family and friends offers excellent opportunities for activities to show love for others. Use children's abilities to plan and work together on projects to further interest and understanding of your church's mission program.

Teachers need to create opportunities for each child to assume increased responsibilities. For example, "Diane, I'd like you and Carol to illustrate these Bible verses in the way you think best. Choose other people in our class to help you if you need them." Should you notice a child needing guidance, give the kind of assistance that will allow him or her to succeed. Ask questions, such as, "Which of these events happened first? . . . What could you do to show that sequence in your mural? . . . Good for you, John and Tom. You've both thought out your project very well!"

Ten- and Eleven-Year-Old Children ■ The ten-year-old has several centers for social activities. While still enjoying family relationships and valuing the judgments and feelings of parents, the ten is strongly influenced by what peers think, feel and do. Friendships and activities with age-mates flourish. These children draw together and away from adults in their desire for independence.

The ten-year-old wants to be part of the group. However, the child does not like to be involved in competition that would result in standing apart from peers. The ability to make valuable contributions to group activities is a beneficial experience. The child participates happily and with success in groups beyond the family cluster.

The eleven-year-old continues to value group activities and is interested in maintaining the group code of behavior. As these preteen years conclude, the child is increasingly critical of adults. A growing lack of willingness to communicate openly is a concern for both teachers and parents. Often the demands for independence are unrealistic.

Because most of these fifth and sixth graders no longer think aloud, keeping communication open is of prime importance for teachers. Make the most of each opportunity for conversation by listening thoughtfully and objectively. Avoid being judgmental! Ask questions to be sure you understand the child's viewpoint.

Intellectual Growth

Six and Seven-Year-Old Children ■ An intense eagerness to learn is a delightful and important characteristic of the six-year-old. This child asks innumerable questions and frequently tries to answer them through experimentation and discovery. Even though the attention span is short, the child enjoys the feelings of security in repeating stories and activities. A limited concept of time and space requires the child to think in terms of here and now, rather than of the past or future.

Listening and speaking skills develop rapidly during this year. Although a child's reading skills are also increasing, the child still is learning to read rather than reading to learn. Generally, girls are ahead of boys, demonstrating longer attention spans and more conversational skills.

A six-year-old tends to focus on only one feature (often insignificant) of an object or a situation. For instance, when looking at a Bible story picture, the child may be fascinated with the unusual garments worn by the people rather than their actions or facial expressions. The first grader shows interest in the parts of a situation rather than seeing the parts in relationship to the whole. When asked what he liked about his father, a boy told of special things his father did for him (fixed his bike, let him help paint the garage) rather than thinking of the qualities of his father's personality, such as his loving and kind nature.

Sixes and sevens think in very literal terms. These children need to see visual illustrations of the words you use. Bible story pictures and figures are essential to their understanding of Bible times and people, and of present-day situations. Symbolistic terms continue to be beyond their understanding.

When planning Bible learning experiences for first or second graders, teachers need to consider the children's skill and ability level. For example, include reading and writing activities for children who enjoy them. For children whose word skills are limited (or nonexistent), include Bible learning experiences involving art and/or music. It is not easy to keep Bible learning exciting and challenging for children. It requires prayer, planning and work to provide Bible learning experiences that fit a child's capabilities and interests.

Eight- and Nine-Year-Old Children ■ During their elementary school years, children gradually acquire the ability to see things from another's viewpoint while retaining their own. Repeated opportunities with other children compel a child to take into account their feelings and attitudes. Third and fourth graders are beginning to realize there may be more than one answer to a question, more than one idea about a given subject and more than one opinion expressed in a discussion. During these elementary years the child begins to become a "reasoning" person. One girl reasoned, "Paul and his friends got to shore because they held onto boards and boards float."

Seeing parts in terms of a whole also begins to evidence itself in a child's thinking. Rather than considering boys, girls, men and women only as separate groups, an elementary child can perceive them as people.

This age child enjoys looking up information and discovering answers to problems and questions. These children are full of questions. They want to know more about Bible characters than just surface information.

Creativity is high in the eight-year-old. Art, music and drama experiences help internalize Bible information that encourages Christian living.

Learning games interest the eight-year-old. As the child is exposed to an increased number of experiences, his or her interest span widens. Concepts of time, space and distance are increasing, making it easier to relate to the past and to the future, as well as to the present.

The communication skills of the eight-year-old are developing at a rapid rate. Individual differences among children can result in rapid progress for some readers and limited progress for others. Both eight- and nine-year-olds are interested in using their newly developed skills to read portions of the Bible. While their ability to talk surpasses their ability to read, they sometimes use words without understanding their meanings.

The intellectual development of these third and fourth graders allows them to accurately group and classify information. For example, a child can grasp divisions in the Bible (the books of the law, poetry, minor prophets, etc.). Map work and looking up information to discover likenesses and differences are now within their ability and interest.

These years are often called the "golden years of memory" because of the ease with which many children memorize. It is imperative that teachers make sure children understand the material they memorize. For example, after a child has repeated a Bible verse, say, "What is another way to say that verse," or, "I'd like you to draw a picture of what that verse means."

To help children move beyond mere learning of facts, teachers need to accompany verbal presentations with Bible related activity. James warned all Christians, "Do not merely listen to the word, and so deceive yourselves. Do what it says" (Jas. 1:22). The more a child can experience, the less danger of misunderstanding or settling for information only there will be.

The child from seven to eleven learns most effectively when doing something to objects, ideas and symbols. This stage of development also requires dealing with personal relationships as well as factual information. For maximum learning, involve the child in the learning process!

Ten- and Eleven-Year-Old Children ■ Generally ten-year-olds are very verbal. Consistently include opportunities for talking, questioning and discussing in your sessions. Ten-year-olds continue to be creative persons. They are able to express ideas and feelings through poetry, songs, drama, stories, drawing and painting.

The ten-year-old is anxious to know the reasons for right and wrong. Making ethical decisions becomes a challenging task. The child is eager to make right choices, but needs your understanding and thoughtful help and guidance without too much specific direction.

Abstract thinking and generalizations are still difficult for some ten-year-olds to understand. Generally they continue to deal best with concepts through firsthand experiences.

Around the age of eleven, the ability to reason abstractly begins to emerge. The child is able to foresee the end result of a situation. Intellectual growth is balanced by continued enjoyment in creating stories, poems, dramas and working creatively with art materials. Role-playing is a helpful means of identifying with different points of view or of practicing the application of truth to life situations.

The eleven-year-old begins to think he or she is becoming an adult. This view brings about serious questioning of adult concepts while at the same time the eleven-year-old is making strides in being able to determine things independently. Adult leadership must be available, but given in such a way that it will not destroy the child's efforts in becoming a thinking, self-directed person. The eleven-year-old is capable of thinking things through and accepting logical conclusions.

As the child becomes more keenly aware of feelings, desires and capabilities, definite ideas about the future begin to develop. Thoughts about a future career, mate and life-style are common parts of daily activity. These preteen years are critical in the growth pattern of a child. The roots of many important decisions are implanted at this age. Hero worship is strong. God often becomes an influence in choices that are being made for the thinking and planning of the future. The concern, understanding and guidance of Christian adults is extremely important in these formative years.

Our tens and elevens continue to have many of the same needs as the sixes, sevens, eights and nines. All need to feel the love and understanding of concerned adults. Learning opportunities need to include involvement, action and discovery. Although tens and elevens are able to absorb Bible facts, their learning is not complete unless they translate these facts into their day-by-day experiences.

Spiritual Growth

At each age level, a generally consistent pattern of development is quite evident in the physical, emotional, social and intellectual dimensions of each child's personality. By comparison, the spiritual dimension of these same children may present a rather inconsistent picture. For example, two children in the same Sunday School class may have had such diverse backgrounds that one grasps the basic concept of God as Spirit while the other has absolutely no concept at all in this area. Therefore, understanding a child's spiritual characteristics requires a careful consideration of personal experiences and Christian training. Generally, children who attend Christian schools, after-school Christian clubs and whose parents are active Christians possess a greater spiritual awareness and understanding than children without these advantages. The child from a non-Christian home may have been exposed to ideas and attitudes that distort scriptural truths.

As you consider the following spiritual characteristics, think of the information in terms of *individual* children in your class rather than the children as a group.

Six- and Seven-Year-Old Children ■ A child who is six or seven years old can sense the greatness, wonder and love of God when these concepts are translated into specific terms within personal experience. For instance, telling a child "God made the world" isn't nearly as meaningful as displaying nature objects that can be examined and used in simple experiments.

The nonphysical nature of God baffles children. However, they accept the concept of God's omnipresence, generally because the significant adults in their lives (parents and teachers) communicate this belief by their words, attitudes and actions.

A child of six or seven can think of the Lord Jesus as a friend who loves and cares for him or her. However, because the concepts of love and care are abstract, a child needs to have these ideas interpreted in literal terms. For example, it helps a child to know that God expresses His love and care by planning that a family would care for each child.

A primary-age child's need to think in literal rather than symbolic terms rules out using such songs as "Jesus Wants Me for a Sunbeam" and "This Little Light of Mine." Abstractions like these are more apt to confuse scriptural concepts than clarify them for a child.

A child responds positively to the idea of talking to God anywhere, anytime and in normal words. Because a youngster's ability to verbalize his thoughts is increasing, praying aloud can become a natural expression of gratitude or petition.

Teachers need to model short sentence prayers, and provide frequent and regular opportunities for children to pray in small groups. Be sure children understand that God in His wisdom will answer a prayer in the way He knows is best.

Each child's independent use of the Bible depends largely on reading skills. The child is not yet able to understand much Bible chronology beyond knowing that the Old Testament happened before Jesus came; that the New Testament tells of Jesus' coming, His work on earth and events that occurred after Jesus went back to heaven. A child's increasing attention span and interest in stories containing action and dialogue make listening to well-told Bible stories a Sunday morning highlight.

The gospel of God's love becomes real as the child feels love from adults. Teachers who demonstrate their faith in a consistent, loving way become channels through which the loving nature of God is made known to a child.

Eight- and Nine-Year-Old Children ■ Understanding that God is all-wise, all-knowing and loving can become part of the child's beliefs and feelings during the elementary school years. Believing God loves and cares for him or her as an important and valued individual helps to increase the child's developing self-esteem.

Learning to make choices and decisions based upon the biblical concept of right and wrong is important at this time in a child's life. Often it is difficult for a child to admit wrongdoing. We can give encouragement by thoughtfully sharing the loving, forgiving nature of God. We can also help the child know God tells us to forgive others as God has forgiven us.

We see our eight- and nine-year-old beginning to sense a need for God's continuous help and guidance. Therefore, we need to assist in developing an understanding and assurance of God's love and answer to prayer. It is often difficult for children of this age to know that God's answer to prayer is always best.

Eight- and nine-year-olds can recognize their need for a personal Savior. They desire to become a member of God's family. Children who indicate an awareness of sin and a concern about accepting the Lord Jesus as Savior need to be carefully guided without pressure from peers or adults. Talk personally with a child whom you sense the Holy Spirit is leading to trust the Lord

Jesus. Ask simple questions (requiring more than a yes or no answer) to determine the child's level of understanding. (See the steps for guiding a child to become a member of God's family suggested in chapter 5.)

Ten- and Eleven-Year-Old Children ■ The ten-year-old is capable of deep feelings of love for God. Often a child of this age naturally shares what he knows about God with a special friend in his peer group. The child is also developing a sense of responsibility to the church. This may include the desire to attend worship service, to accept some responsibility for work within the church, or to be involved in evangelism and service projects.

Because a ten-year-old is usually comfortable in reading skills, this is an ideal time to encourage reading the Bible regularly and to complete specific assignments. For example, a learner may read specific passages, then list five ways God showed His love for Moses.

A ten-year-old is able to bring increased skill, reasoning and a widening background of experience to Bible learning. The child is beginning to understand and appreciate symbolism, and is on the threshold of moving from concrete to abstract understanding of concepts. This child is able to incorporate pieces of information and ideas from earlier learning into broader principles, rather than being confined to the simplistic, single idea thinking of younger years. For instance, a six grader's concept of sin is apt to include "doing things that are hurtful to oneself and others and displeasing to God," while a second grader's concept of sin generally is limited to not obeying God.

Leading a Child to Christ

Many older elementary age children are able to grasp the relationship between God's love, His forgiveness and our hope for eternal life. They are aware of their need for God's forgiveness and a need for a personal Savior. When you feel the Holy Spirit is speaking to a child, make opportunities to talk with him or her. Ask thoughtful questions that will help express his or her understanding and feelings about God. (Later in this chapter see suggestions for guiding a child to become a member of God's family.)

Deciphering symbolic and allegorical material is a challenging and enjoyable experience for many sixth graders. As the child incorporates these figures of speech into creative expressions of art, music, poetry and prose, he or she discovers new insights and relevance in God's Word.

Any consideration of children's spiritual development also requires that we think of the deep impressions our attitudes and actions make upon them. They are tremendously receptive to our modeling of a biblical Christian life-style. When they see a discrepancy between what we say and the way we think and act, then confusion is bound to result in their thinking. However, when our words and deeds consistently reflect a Christian maturity after which to model their lives, then we are reflecting the Christian life as the apostle Paul admonished: "You yourselves are our letter, written on our hearts, known and read by everybody. You show that you are a letter from Christ, the result of our ministry, written not with ink but with the Spirit of the living God, not on tablets of stone but on tablets of human hearts" (2 Cor. 3:2,3).

HOW CAN YOU GUIDE A CHILD TO BECOME A MEMBER OF GOD'S FAMILY?

One of the greatest privileges of serving as a Sunday School teacher is to help children learn how they can become members of God's family.

Some children, especially those from Christian homes, may be ready to believe in Jesus Christ as their Savior earlier than others. Pray that the Holy Spirit will give you wisdom and keep you sensitive to every child's spiritual need. Remember, salvation is a supernatural work of the Holy Spirit and is the result of God speaking to the child. Your role is to guide the child to discover how to become a Christian.

Because children are easily influenced to follow the group, be very cautious about asking for group decisions. Plan opportunities to talk and pray individually with any child who desires to become a member of God's family.

Follow these basic steps in talking simply with the child about how to become a member of God's family. The booklet, *God Wants YOU to Be a Member of His Family,* is an effective guide to follow as you talk and pray with each child.

God Wants You to Grow as His Child is designed for follow-up of children who have prayed to become God's child. Show what God says in His Word as you talk with a child:

"God wants you to become a member of His family. Since He

made you and knows you, He wants you to be a part of His family. Of course, you are a member of your own family. Some of us have large families with a mom and dad and sisters and brothers. Some of us have much smaller families, but all of us have people who love and take care of us. You know what it is to be a part of a family. God wants you to be a part of His family and to live and grow as His child.

"How do you become a member of God's family? There are a few steps that you need to take to become His child. Let's look at them."

Step One: God Loves You.
"The Bible says in 1 John 4:8 that 'God is love.' He loves you very much. He loved you enough to make you and He keeps up with you every day.

Step Two: You Have Sinned.
"The Bible also says that you and other people have sinned. In Romans 3:23 you can read, *'All have sinned and fall short of the glory of God.'*

"You have done wrong things. We all have done wrong things. Sometimes we cheat on a test. Sometimes we steal something from a friend. Some of us tell lies. Some of us don't show respect to our parents. The Bible's word for doing any wrong is sin.

"Sin keeps you from being friends with God. Sin always leads to trouble. Because you are a sinner, your sin will cause much trouble in your life. Romans 6:23 tells us how bad this trouble will be: *'For the wages of sin is death, but the free gift of God is eternal life through Jesus Christ our Lord'* (TLB).

"God does not want people to ruin their lives with sin. It makes Him very sad when you do wrong things and spoil your happiness and the happiness of other people. People who sin also cannot go to live with God in heaven. Maybe you think the things you do aren't so bad. Maybe you think doing something wrong is okay as long as you don't get caught. God knows about the bad things you do. He even knows when you are thinking about doing something wrong. Everybody does bad things, even the people who look like they always behave themselves. Not one of us is good enough to go to heaven without some very special help from God Himself."

Step Three: God Paid the Price.
"In the beginning of the Bible there is the story of Adam and Eve, the first people. The Bible tells us that Adam and Eve lived happily with God until they disobeyed Him. That was the first sin. One of the results of the sin was that someday Adam and Eve would grow old and die. All of us sin, so someday each of us will die.

"There is another life after we die. If we have sinned, we have to be punished in a terrible place. If we have never sinned at all, we get to go to heaven to be with God. You already know that everybody sins, so how does anybody get to go to heaven?

"The Bible says in Romans 6:23, *'For the wages of sin is death, but the free gift of God is eternal life through Christ Jesus our Lord' (TLB)*. Yes, the wages of sin is death. It is our punishment for being a sinner. Bad things have been done, and somebody has to pay for them! However, because God loves you so much, He paid the price for your sin already! He bought you with a great price! How did He do it?

"He gave His only Son to die for you on the cross. The Bible says, in 1 Corinthians 15:3, *'Christ died for our sins according to the Scriptures.'* Because Jesus was the perfect Man—without sin (He is God) He could be punished in your place. He paid the price for your sin. The Bible says in 1 John 4:14, *'The Father has sent his Son to be the Savior of the world.'*

"Imagine, God loves you so much and He knows you so well that He gave His Son to die for you! How does that make you feel? Are you sad because of your sin? Are you glad because of this good news?"

Step Four: Ask God for His Forgiveness.

"Are you sorry for your sin? Do you believe that God gave His only Son to pay for your sins with His life? Do you believe that God paid the price for you?

"If you believe this, then tell God you believe He gave His Son, Jesus Christ, to take your punishment. Also tell God you know you are a sinner. Tell Him that He is a great and wonderful God. It is easy to talk to God. Just call His name and He will be ready to listen. What you are going to tell Him is something He has been waiting to hear.

"If you believe, now you are a child of God! God has forgiven all your sin.

"Do you know what happens when God forgives you? He makes everything right between you and Him. He has forgiven you and He looks upon you as if you had never sinned! Imagine, your God did this for you!"

Step Five: You Are His Child.

"Now you are God's child. You are a member of His family. The Bible says in John 1:12, *'But as many as received Him, to them He gave the right to become children of God, even to those who believe in His name'* (NASB). As a child of God you receive God's gift of everlasting life. This means God is with you now and forever.

"Maybe you had a grandmother or grandfather who died, or maybe you had a friend your own age who died. Someday you will die, too. Maybe your body will get worn out or sick. Maybe you will get badly hurt in an accident before you grow up. Nobody knows when he or she will die.

"Did you ever wonder or worry about what happens when you die? When you die as a child of God, you will go to heaven and be given a brand new body even better than the old one. Jesus even has a special place ready for you to live. You will never have to worry about what happens when you die, because now you are a child of God. Isn't that good news? The Bible says in John 3:16, *'For God so loved the world, that He gave His only begotten Son, that whoever believes in Him should not perish, but have eternal life' (NASB)."*

Step Six: Live as God's Child.
"Now that you are a member of God's family, God wants you to live as His child. Because you are His child, He wants you to do certain things.

You Can Talk to God
"Because God is your heavenly Father, He wants you to talk to Him. This is called prayer. You can tell God that you love Him. You can thank Him for loving you. You can also ask God to help you live as His child. The Bible says (Ps. 143:10), *'Teach me to do your will, for you are my God.'*

"You can also talk to God when you sin. You will still do wrong things. But now, you can ask God to forgive you and He will. The Bible says, in 1 John 1:9, *'If we confess our sins, He is faithful and righteous to forgive us our sins and to cleanse us from all unrighteousness' (NASB).* God will forgive you and help you do what He says."

You Can Read God's Word
"God gave His Word so that everyone can read about Him and His great love. You can know what God says by reading about Him in your Bible. The Bible says, *Your word I have treasured in my heart that I might not sin against you* (see Ps. 119:11). You read God's Word to stay close to Him. It's just like reading a letter from a person you really love. You read the letter over and over again. We do the same thing with our Bible."

You Can Obey God
"Your heavenly Father wants you to obey Him. He tells you in His Word what you should do to live as His child.

You need to:
Obey Mom and Dad.
Show kindness.
Be honest and fair.
Help anyone who needs you.
Read God's Word.
Pray to Him.
Tell others about Jesus."

You Can Tell Your Friends About Jesus

"Jesus said in Acts 1:8, *'You will be my witnesses.'* Jesus was talking to His disciples before He went back to His Father. Even though Jesus was talking to His disciples, He was saying these words to you, too. You are a witness when you tell others about Jesus.

"Because you are a child of God you will want to tell others about what Jesus did for you. Plan to talk with one or two friends about Jesus this week. Pick a quiet time when you and your friends can be serious. Tell them about what you have done. Take the *God Wants YOU to Be a Member of His Family* booklet. Start with Step One. Tell your friends about God's love. Go through the rest of the steps until you have asked your friends to become part of God's family too! If you do this whenever you can, God's family will grow!"

You may find it necessary to lead the child in a prayer of confession. If so, also encourage the child to talk personally to God.

Follow this prayer time with brief moments of conversation to clarify the decision. Remember to encourage and pray for the child frequently, and provide for additional spiritual nurturing.

If you use the *God Wants YOU* booklet, the student may sign it and keep it in his or her Bible as a record of this decision to believe in the Lord Jesus. Explain that the child should read the booklet again and again. It has the verses that you read together. The book tells where to find other Bible verses that teach what to do now.

Encourage the child to tell his or her parents about this decision. Arrange to talk with the parents about the child's decision. They may be interested in seeing a copy of the *God Wants YOU* booklet and the biblical steps in becoming a member of God's family you used in talking with their child. Be alert to the Holy Spirit's working in the heart of a parent who may also be ready to become a child of God. Remember that your ministry with children includes their families as well.

PART 2

The Dynamics of Learning

Children's Learning Styles

As you prepare your lesson material week after week do you sometimes wonder, "Are the children really learning what I'm teaching? How can I know?"

To answer these questions, we need to ask, "How do children learn? Is there more than one way to learn? What is meant by the learning process? What do I need to know about the learning process to be an effective teacher?"

Let's think about the implications of these questions for a child's Christian education as we consider the process called learning.

ONE STYLE OF TEACHING AND LEARNING

Think back to the way you were taught in Sunday School. What kind of learning opportunities did your teachers provide?

Traditionally, teachers in the church education program viewed their role as preparing a lesson and presenting it in such a way as to captivate and maintain the attention of their students. In this procedure the student was primarily passive—sitting, listening and watching the teacher and from time to time asking or answering questions. The teacher was by far the most active since he or she had studied, prepared and presented the lesson. How many times have we heard a teacher say, "I've learned so much by studying for this!"? The teacher seemed to be the one learning the most since the teacher was the one participating in the tasks or activities. The teacher was at the center of the learning process while the learners were at the perimeter.

When the teacher's role is to be a teller or dispenser of information, the student is generally relegated to the lesser, passive role of listener. The learner is expected to soak up information and at appropriate times ask questions and discuss matters pertaining to the lesson.

This teaching style is called the "mug-jug" theory of education. Basically, this theory pictures the teacher as the "mug" and the student as the "jug." Education is simplified to the process of the "mug" pouring knowledge into the "empty jug."

Research in public education has shown that from 50 to 75 percent of a child's time in the classroom is spent listening. This fact indicates that teachers talk too much and children talk too little! The percentage of time a child spends listening in the Sunday School may be even higher!

Another significant factor related to the "mug-jug" theory in education is physical in nature. In this setting the student is expected to sit still most of the time—something contrary to a child's stage of development. Sitting still may require so much effort on a child's part that it is impossible to concentrate on learning!

ANOTHER VIEW

Children develop a life-style strikingly similar to the significant adults (parents, friends, teachers) around which they have centered their lives and activities. If the ultimate objective of a Bible teaching ministry is for each child "to be conformed to the likeness of his Son" (Rom. 8:29), then it is the teacher's own Christlikeness that will serve as a model to direct each child's mind and heart toward the living Lord Jesus.

"Follow my example, as I follow the example of Christ," the apostle Paul told the Corinthians (1 Cor. 11:1). Paul repeatedly presented this dynamic concept of modeling as essential to Christian growth. A child must see the reality of Christ in the attitudes and actions of his teacher.

The teacher needs to view his or her role in partnership with the Holy Spirit. For it is by His Spirit that a teacher is enabled to not only model Christlikeness, but also to lead children in each part of the learning process. In this setting a teacher:

a. accepts, clarifies and supports the ideas and feelings of students

b. praises and encourages each learner for efforts as well as achievements

c. asks questions to stimulate a student to discover truths from God's Word

d. provides opportunities for learners to participate in decision making.

CONTENT

Historically, Sunday Schools have majored on Bible content; after all, teaching the life-transforming Word of God is the primary purpose of these institutions. However, in this vital task, many teachers concentrate on the factual and historical content of the Word almost to the exclusion of its realistic application to students' everyday needs. In Sunday Schools where this imbalance between content and application exists, the "mug-jug" style of teaching usually predominates. Emphasis in this approach is restricted to transferring biblical data from the teacher to the student; not upon helping the student in a variety of ways discover and make practical use of this same information.

"All Scripture is God-breathed and is useful for teaching, rebuking, correcting and training in righteousness, so that the man of God may be thoroughly equipped for every good work" (2 Tim. 3:16, 17). Clearly, according to Scripture, the teaching of the Word should result in changed lives. When the content of teaching is selected for its relevance to the understanding and development of the student, and when the method of teaching includes a variety of proven learning methods, the Holy Spirit's unique working in the student's mind and heart becomes evident by Christian growth.

INDIVIDUAL LEARNING STYLES

Traditionally, we instructed our children as if they all learned the same way; therefore we taught them all the same way. Today we know that to expect all children at a given age or grade to learn the same way, at the same rate, and to do the same quality work is as unrealistic as expecting them all to wear the same size clothing.

Some children learn best when an inductive approach is used—studying the various parts of a Bible character's life and finally arriving at some generalizations about the character. Other children will benefit more from a deductive pattern—moving from a particular truth or principle to its various parts and relationships. Some children learn Bible truths best through firsthand experiences, through the use of their senses. Most children learn more when their efforts are spaced over several short periods of time, in a series of Sunday sessions. Others can learn effectively in a concentrated period or block of time during which they can thoroughly absorb what is being taught.

Basis for Individual Differences

A child's preferences for learning in specific ways is based, to some degree, upon past learning experiences. But there are also some deeper bases for individual learning differences. These differences cannot be significantly modified by the teacher. Rather, the teacher must modify the programs according to these variations and individual makeup in order to bring about effective learning for each individual.

There are four basic contributors to individual differences.

The first basis of individual differences is simple, organic variation. Each person's body contains organs of varying size, shape, location and rates of functioning. Thus, all of the organs that enter into the constitution of the human body vary from individual to individual. The brain, heart, stomach, lungs and the glands, which contribute to the person's functioning, all reveal considerable individual differences in students. These differences affect a child's learning abilities.

Second, every child differs from others in past experiences. Both the satisfying experiences and the dissatisfying experiences will affect the child's attitude and response in a particular learning situation. The child who has found Sunday School to be extremely boring will come to class clouded with the memory of these previous negative experiences and will be a particular challenge to any Sunday School teacher.

Those children who are brought into Sunday School through a church's bus ministry are frequently void of any experiences in the realm of Christianity. Other children will come who have had religious experiences in a nominal Christian home where they have learned to pray and include God in some of their conversations, but with no reality in evidence.

A number of children may have accepted Christ as Savior within their homes, in a class or at a camp. Many other children will not have even heard of the significance of this experience. Our teaching methods need to take into account the variety of student experiences present in the classroom.

The differing amount of information that students have acquired on various subjects is the third basis for individual differences. Those students who come from a Christian home where Christian education takes place each day will be well oriented in Christian vocabulary and in the knowledge of basic Bible stories. The student who has received no home instruction will be totally dependent upon the information received through Christian friends and through Sunday School.

A fourth basis of individual differences is group membership and interpersonal relationships. A student who has brothers and sisters can more easily adjust to a group of students within a Sunday School class than children who lack such interaction. Children who lack wholesome relationships, or who have had few opportunities to develop interpersonal relationships, will require more help and attention in adjusting to the group learning climate. Many older children will have had some type of group membership, in a scouting program, school activity or community club organization. The social experience with adults as well as peers of each child will vary greatly and will affect the group learning experiences of the children as well as their adjustment to the authority figures in the classroom.

Effectiveness in teaching children often breaks down when our plan for all students is the same. Variety and flexibility are two essential words in every teacher's vocabulary.

THE INTERPLAY OF SIMILARITY AND UNIQUENESS

Although there are obvious differences among individual children, there are enough basic similarities so we can design an educational plan to meet the needs of large numbers of children.

And although there are similarities in human development, children are unique individuals. All children do not move through various growth stages in a lock-step fashion. There is an interplay between similarity and uniqueness among our children. This interplay poses a fascinating challenge for Sunday School teachers: How do we deal with groups of children in ways that allow us to meet each child's individual needs?

SUMMARY

All children do not fit into a rigid pattern of instruction; God has made them unique and thus incompatible with inflexible patterns. Although we can understand the general stages children are passing through, we also know that we will have to take into account their distinct differences—physically, experientially, socially and intellectually. Our instruction needs to begin where the students are and build upon the students' experience and information in order to bring them to greater spiritual understanding. We must see that what we teach is appropriate for the various stages of development and individual differences represented in our classroom. We need to be open to effective learning methods, which can serve as a basis for learning and experiencing God's revelation through the teaching ministry of the Holy Spirit.

Five Steps to Dynamic Learning

Ministering effectively to children requires that we understand the basic steps in a child's learning process. Then we need to plan Bible teaching/learning experiences with an awareness of this process.

Let's begin by looking at five basic learning steps essential to dynamic learning in Christian education.

LISTENING

An essential learning task is listening or giving attention. It is the initial point of contact for the teacher seeking to initiate the learning process. Securing the attention of children is strategic; it involves motivating the student through the combined influence of the room environment (see chapter 9) and initial introduction to the material to be studied. For example, using a puppet to give directions for a particular learning experience is an effective way to catch children's attention. Attractively-displayed learning materials (open Bible, ruled paper, sharpened pencils, directions lettered on colorful stand-up cards, etc.) also gain a child's attention and "want to" at the beginning of a learning experience.

EXPLORING

The second step in the learning process, exploring, involves the careful investigation of a problem or subject. The student is an explorer, totally involved in the search for something not yet known or experienced. The learner is not a mere spectator but a central and active participant in the learning process.

Generally, this type of learning results from observing the following principles:

1. At some points in every session, children may select an activity (all of which are lesson-related) in which they would like to participate. Such a procedure recognizes that children have different interests and talents as well as varying abilities in learning. At times some children may prefer and learn best from art-learning projects, while others may profit most from music or research projects.

2. Children may help determine the manner in which they will pursue an activity with respect to the materials and activities available.

3. Children may collaborate with their fellow students in a learning activity. Such cooperation encourages and extends learning, since the children tend to stimulate each other as they progress in the exploration of the subject matter.

4. Children can be trusted by their teachers. The principle that guides these teachers is, "I can trust this child until he gives me reason not to, and then I will be more cautious about trusting him in that particular area."

5. Children need a classroom environment where there is consistent order and the comparison of student performance is minimized.

DISCOVERING

As a result of the listening and exploring processes the learner discovers what the Bible says. Then, guided by the Holy Spirit, the learner understands its implications for his or her own life.

Discovering God's eternal truths in His Word is an exciting process. Too often the teacher is the only one who makes these discoveries. Although a teacher may excitedly share them with the students, why shouldn't the joy of discovery also be the child's? Discovery does not require leaving the child to flounder in hopes he or she will stumble upon something, for the teacher is present to carefully lead the process.

APPROPRIATING

A child needs to understand the personal implications of God's Word. Recognizing that the Bible has personal meaning, builds confidence in Scripture as "an ever present help" (Ps.46:1).

There are many ways to guide the child's task of appropriating. The teacher may pose a real problem to solve on the basis of a biblical truth. For example, Bill loved baseball and was playing the last inning when he realized that it was past dinnertime. He knew his parents would be waiting for him but he didn't want to leave the game. What should he do? What does the Bible tell us about this kind of problem? Or, use an open-end story for the children to complete. For example, "Steve asked Carol if he could copy her homework and Carol decided . . . because . . . "

As a result of this step in the learning process, the child knows what God expects in situations related to this truth. However, the end of the learning process has not been reached because the student has not yet put the lesson truth into action in personal experience.

ASSUMING RESPONSIBILITY

This is the crown of the learning process, the place where the previous tasks—listening, exploring, discovering and appropriating—culminate. Here God's truth actually changes and molds a child's thinking, attitude and behavior. This final learning task is of great significance. For it is at this point that our efforts to effectively communicate God's truth should result in changed lives. Our children must perceive the necessity of doing certain things on the basis of what they have been experiencing (in the previous steps of the learning process). A child needs to see clearly the actions necessitated by the study and be led into assuming responsibility for them.

Even when a child makes a practical application of a Scripture truth, learning does not stop there. The child continues to form new perceptions and compare them with old ones. The child solves new problems on the basis of these fresh insights. The true test of learning comes when a child voluntarily uses learning in new situations.

The process of learning is summed up in these five steps. Listening, exploring, discovering, appropriating and assuming responsibility are not simply activities in which students are to be engaged but are inseparably bound together with Christian goals and objectives. Through the Holy Spirit's guidance of a thoughtful teacher, the spiritual dimension of a child's personality can continue its growth and development.

"And Jesus grew in wisdom and stature, and in favor with God and men" (Luke 2:52).

SUMMARY

What are the practical implications for these steps of the learning process? How does this information affect leaders' and teachers' preparation?

There is an inherent progression in the first four learning steps—listening, exploring, discovering and appropriating. They spiral upward, even though the cycle is often broken and frequently repeated. Two processes cut through the spiral. The first process is the fifth learning step, that of assuming responsibility. The second is a process distinctive to Christian education—the intervention of the Holy Spirit, who uses the truth of God's Word to transform people's lives!

During a typical Sunday morning, through the processes of Bible exploration, and Bible Learning Activities, children should be actively involved in these steps of the learning process. Teachers and leaders need to understand the dynamic interrelationship of these steps and allow time for their completion. Instruction is not the mere transmission of biblical information to the students but rather the personal participation of each student in a creative study of God's Word. Within this context, students have the opportunity to develop personally in their spiritual understanding and growth.

Conditions for Dynamic Learning

MOTIVATION

There is a direct relationship between motivation to learn and the effectiveness of the learning process. How can we motivate children to want to learn?

Consider these suggestions for motivating children. Although not every idea will be effective with every child, never give up! As long as communication between teacher and student exists, there is an opportunity for increasing a child's motivation to participate and to learn.

1. Know your learners. Never can this concept be overemphasized. Become well acquainted with each child in your class to know individual interests, abilities and skills. Your insights will enable you to increase motivation for participation and learning by helping the child to recognize abilities, utilize skills and respond to areas of personal interest. Very often a seemingly unmotivated student will gladly participate in activities that relate to his or her interests and abilities.

2. Plan for children to consistently have a choice of activities within limits. When a child is allowed to choose between equally acceptable options, the act of choosing is in itself a way of increasing interest. Allowing choices of ways to complete an activity (e.g. deciding on use of chalk, paint or crayons for a mural) also increases interest and motivation.

3. Provide opportunities for children to interact with each other. Most children respond favorably to working together in small groups, in pairs or in the total group. As interaction increases so does motivation.

4. Listen attentively. An adult who listens to what a child has to say provides motivation and incentive for that child to cooperate and participate in learning experiences.

5. Be flexible in your teaching procedure. Too much predictability leads to boredom for both children and teachers. Although a program needs stability, at the same time a viable program has a balance of change and flexibility.

6. Provide opportunities for children to help other people. For example, a service project catches the imagination and enthusiasm of children as a firsthand experience to put God's Word into action.

Constantly explore methods of increasing motivation. Each child wants to succeed and do what is expected. The child wants to learn. These desires, together with appropriate motivation by you, should insure effective interest and learning.

EMOTIONAL CLIMATE

The emotional climate or feeling level of a classroom is another significant factor in the learning process. Think about your class as you consider these questions:

- How does each child feel about being present?
- Do both you and the children look forward to studying God's Word together as one of the highlights of the week?
- Does each child feel your acceptance and support?
- Is there an atmosphere of warmth and happiness?
- Is there an opportunity for each learner to succeed?
- Are choices provided?
- Is there a feeling of love and trust?
- Do room arrangement and decor make it a pleasant place?
- How do you insure a relaxed pace, free from time pressure?
- How are you helping children build relationships with one another?
- Do you include time for listening to your learners?

- Are your expectations of children realistic and consistent?
- How is the Bible truth being made relevant and alive to the children?

Do these ideas sound overwhelming? Check the list again. Mark the ones that are now an integral part of your classroom procedure or environment. Look at the others. Give them a priority rating. Work on one at a time. For example, experiment with different ways to express praise and recognition to children (see chapter 4). Do what is most comfortable for you. As you begin to feel relaxed and comfortable, so will your learners.

Each teacher is a different individual just as each learner is different. As you become increasingly aware of the emotional climate in your classroom, you will find an increasing number of ways to make it a good place for you and your children to be!

A CONTINUOUS PROCESS

Learning is a continuing process that begins at birth and does not stop until death. A child is learning something—good or bad, right or wrong—every waking moment. Think about this concept as you consider "Children Learn What They Live" by Dorothy Law Nolte.[1]

Children Learn What They Live

If a child lives with criticism,
he learns to condemn . . .
If a child lives with hostility,
he learns to fight . . .
If a child lives with fear,
he learns to be apprehensive . . .
If a child lives with pity,
he learns to feel sorry for himself . . .
If a child lives with ridicule,
he learns to be shy . . .
If a child lives with jealousy,
he learns what envy is . . .

If a child lives with shame,
he learns to feel guilty . . .
If a child lives with encouragement,
he learns to be confident . . .
If a child lives with tolerance,
he learns to be patient . . .
If a child lives with praise,
he learns to be appreciative . . .
If a child lives with acceptance,
he learns love . . .
If a child lives with approval,
he learns to like himself . . .
If a child lives with recognition,
he learns that it is good to have a goal . . .
If a child lives with sharing,
he learns about generosity . . .
If a child lives with honesty and fairness,
he learns what truth and justice are . . .
If a child lives with security,
he learns to have faith in himself and in those about him . . .
If a child lives with friendliness,
he learns that the world is a nice place in which to live . . .
If you live with serenity,
your child will live with peace of mind . . .

The years of childhood are filled with efforts to find a place of belonging. As a child is helped to feel secure and loved, it becomes possible for the child to respect and love others. In order to grow as God intends, a child needs to be nurtured by people who have experienced God's love, and who can help the child receive God's love through Jesus Christ—for "while we were still sinners, Christ died for us" (Rom. 5:8).

A GUIDE TO DISCIPLINE

What is the question most frequently asked by teachers about children?

"How do I maintain discipline?"
"How do I get children to behave properly?"
"What do I do when they get out of control?"
"What about the disruptive child?"

Fortunately, there are some guidelines to help answer questions concerning discipline. However, the answers really depend on teachers recognizing the relationship between the two dimensions of the word *discipline*—guidance and punishment.

Unfortunately, many people use the words *discipline* and *punishment* synonymously. In so doing they miss the primary meaning of the word. Discipline is the process of providing guidance. Discipline primarily concerns itself with helping a child acquire self-control—inner commitment to do what is right. To make punishment the focus of the word is almost like making the street sweeping crews the stars of the parade instead of filling the intended role of following the main attraction, correcting problems and putting things back in order.

Preventing Behavior Problems

"An ounce of prevention . . . . " How much better for children when things go well and episodes of misbehavior and punishment are avoided! Consider the following ideas to make Sunday School "a good place to be" on Sunday mornings.

■ *Develop an atmosphere of love and acceptance.* Each child who enters your classroom needs to feel loved and wanted. Children long to feel that someone cares about them; that they are people of value and worth. Sitting down and listening attentively to what a child has to tell, or kindly but firmly redirecting a child's out-of-bounds activity, are but two of many ways to demonstrate your love and care in ways a child can understand. Every child needs to be accepted just that way.

■ *Provide meaningful activities.* Children need to be actively involved in interesting things to do—not just required to listen or observe for the entire session. Children often misbehave simply because they are bored when there is nothing new or challenging to engage their minds.

■ *Set realistic standards that can be enforced.* Be realistic and consistent in what you expect the child to be or to do. For example, recognize that a child's ability to sit still is limited. So provide physical activities and changes of pace in the schedule that allow children to release pent-up energies. Children also need the security of knowing you are consistent in the way you maintain a certain standard of behavior.

In planning Bible learning experiences, establish realistic goals. For example, if a child is unable to learn an entire verse, focus on a portion of the material and thereby achieve success.

■ *Recognize accomplishments and good behavior.* "I really appreciated how you . . . " or "You're really good at . . . " are two ways to affirm your learners. Encourage all students; not only those who are often behavior problems, but also those who have already achieved a high degree of self-control. When children know they will receive attention for positive behavior, their display of disruptive behavior often diminishes.

Correcting Behavior Problems

There are occasions when corrective measures are necessary. In dealing with a behavior challenge, we can do one of two things—ignore it or respond to it. There are times when ignoring the problem will be the best solution. Many children would prefer our negative attention to no attention. Often we are guilty of making an issue of matters that would be better left alone.

When we cannot ignore misbehavior, here are five helpful steps we can follow to correct the situation.

1. *Deal with the problem individually.* To avoid embarrassing the child in front of friends, it is best to talk with him alone.

2. *Have the child tell what he or she did.* Don't ask why the child behaved in that way. A "why" question merely invites the child to attempt justifying the offense. Perhaps you will want to tell what you saw and then ask, "Is that what happened?" Deal only with the current situation. Do not bring up past offenses.

3. *Be sure the child understands why the behavior is not acceptable in the classroom.* Either ask the child to tell why the

action is a problem, or offer a clear explanation of the reason you intervened. Phrase your explanation so the child can recognize the problem as his or her own; that it results in a loss to the individual and to the group.

4. *Re-direct the child into positive behavior.* Focus on good behavior. For example, ask, "Can you think of a better thing you could have done?" or "What can you do about it now?" Then help the child implement positive changes. As the child makes these changes, give honest and sincere praise to reward acceptable behavior.

5. *Let the child experience the consequences of behavior.* If a child puts a hand on a hot stove, a burn results. If a person does not eat, hunger results. When materials are misused in the classroom, we can remove the materials from the child, or we can remove the child from the materials. Let the child choose whether to correct behavior voluntarily or to lose a privilege or some other response appropriate to the offense.

Your positive approach to the needs of your students is one of the most important factors in making your classroom a good place to be. Guiding a child to learn self-control and to demonstrate obedience to parents and teachers is a first step to the ultimate goal of helping the child learn obedience to the Lord. Pray for understanding, wisdom and patience. Be a loving, caring person both inside and outside the classroom, no matter what the behavior challenge may be "If you love someone you will . . . always expect the best of him" (1 Cor. 13:7, TLB).

NOTE

1. Dorothy Law Nolte, "Children Learn What They Live" (Los Angeles: The American Institute of Family Relations, n.d.).

Facilities for Children

A classroom is that silent partner that has the potential to aid or hinder student learning and behavior, to enhance or negate even the best curriculum and teaching methods. Children's classrooms need to reflect order, friendliness and some degree of spaciousness for a variety of learning experiences. Consciously or unconsciously, a learner is influenced by the environment as well as by teachers and peers.

What contributes then to a healthy learning environment for children? How can we improve our classrooms to provide effective learning opportunities for each child?

DESIGNING AN EFFECTIVE FACILITY

Study the Sunday School room plans on the following page. While they may not look exactly like the room in which you teach, there are basic elements in the diagram and in your room that should be similar.

Walls themselves need to absorb sound and be painted in cheerful colors. Research by the American Medical Association has disclosed that children's grades rose noticeably when their rooms were decorated in attractive yellow. Bright colors tend to be stimulating and exciting. They are most effectively used in small areas. Colors such as pale yellow and white suggest sunshine and look well on large wall areas. Use these colors in rooms with northern window exposure. Dark walls can be gloomy and depressing unless well lighted and accented with a light color. Blues and greens create a feeling of coolness, which

DIAGRAM 1

OPEN ROOM ARRANGEMENT

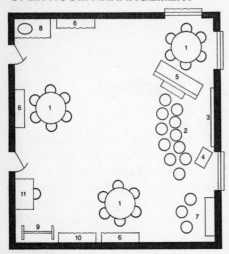

1 ● Table and chairs to seat 6-8 children for Bible study and Bible learning activities.
2 ● Chairs (used at tables) grouped for Bible sharing time.
3 ● Bulletin board with picture rail.
4 ● Small table for leader's materials.
5 ● Piano (optional).
6 ● Low shelves for materials (glue, paper, crayons, etc.).
7 ● Bookshelf with several chairs.
8 ● Storage cabinets and sink counter.
9 ● Coatrack.
10 ● Shelves for take-home materials.
11 ● Secretary's desk.

DIAGRAM 2

ASSEMBLY/CLASSROOM ARRANGEMENT

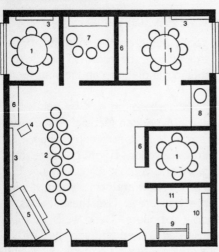

makes them good choices for rooms having southern and western window exposure. Colors can hide undesirable features and emphasize desirable ones. Choose your colors wisely so they are a supportive element in the teaching-learning environment.

Floors and ceilings should be complementary in color and provide sound absorption. White acoustical ceilings are standard in educational building construction.

There is a growing trend toward the use of carpet rather than tile or linoleum in educational facilities. The initial cost of materials and installation is higher but the maintenance of carpet is less costly than that of tile or linoleum, and therefore less expensive in the long run. The most positive contribution of carpet to a children's learning environment is the acoustical value and warmth it provides.

Lighting of children's rooms is very important. Lighting standards for schools have increased over the past 20 years, and architects now recommend increased wattage to provide adequate light for reading and writing activities. Floor, wall and ceiling color can either reflect light or absorb it, so plan accordingly for the color and light wattage in your room. If your room needs extra light, install white window shades. Or, remove existing shades and install light bulbs with higher wattage. (Check first with the maintenance personnel in your church.)

SPACE REQUIREMENTS

Twenty-five to thirty square feet (2.25 to 2.7 sq. meters) of floor space per person should be provided in each children's department. (The recommended maximum attendance in each department is 30.) A department room (or suite of adjoining rooms) with less than 750 square feet will become uncomfortably crowded and limit participation in group activities when attendance reaches 30 children.

Studies in church growth have shown that when a group has grown to occupy 70 percent of its available space, growth strangulation occurs. The room size actually deters further growth.

Since we are working toward the growth of our Sunday Schools, a children's department should be kept at a size where maximum teaching/learning can transpire and numerical growth can be stimulated.

USEFUL EQUIPMENT

For a learning environment to be effective, it is necessary to select materials and equipment with care. Although quality products are generally more costly, the additional investment is extremely worthwhile in terms of long and satisfactory use.

Chairs

The nonfolding type of chair is recommended. A tubular, steel-frame chair with a plastic seat and back, which is stackable, has proved adequate and durable.

Specifications ■ *Grades 1 to 3:* The height (floor to chair seat) should be 12-14 inches (30-35 cm) for first and second graders and 14-15 inches (35-37.5 cm) for third graders.

■ *Grades 4 to 6:* The height should be 14-15 inches (35-37.5 cm) for fourth and fifth graders and 16 inches (40 cm) for sixth graders.

Tables

Tables should comfortably seat eight children and a teacher. Rectangular and trapezoidal tables in the size shown in Diagram 3 are recommended because of their versatility. They may be pushed squarely against the wall to free floor space for other activities or fit together to make a table around which two small groups of children may gather.

The kidney-shaped table is popular because the teacher is physically close to each student. However, this table does not have the versatility of the rectangular table; also the child at the extreme right and left of the teacher has an obstructed view of materials the teacher may show. Long rectangular tables require too much space, are heavy to move and make it difficult for the students to work together. Round tables are generally more expensive than rectangular ones, are more difficult to place out of the way than a rectangular table. Also, when the table is full, children's papers are liable to overlap, causing possible conflicts.

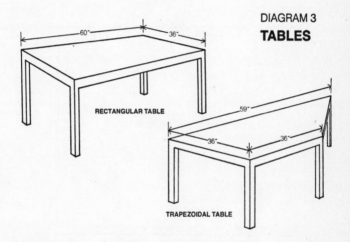

DIAGRAM 3
TABLES

RECTANGULAR TABLE

TRAPEZOIDAL TABLE

Specifications ■ *Grades 1 to 3:* The tabletops should be no smaller than 30×48 inches (75×120 cm) and no larger than 36×60 inches (90×150 cm).

■ *Grades 4 to 6:* The tabletops should be approximately 36×60 inches (90×150 cm).

A table should be 10 inches (25 cm) above chair seat height. Adjustable legs are desirable.

Chalkboard

Older elementary children and their teachers will use a chalkboard more frequently than younger age groups. An assembly room should have a board (permanently installed) approximately 3×5 feet (90×150 cm) or 4×6 feet (120×180 cm) in size. The chalk rail also serves as a picture rail. Small classrooms located off a large assembly room should each have a chalkboard approximately 3 × 5 feet (90 × 150 cm).

Specifications ■ *Grades 1 to 3:* All boards should be placed from 28-30 inches (70-75 cm) above the floor.
Grades 4 to 6: Place boards 32 inches (80 cm) above floor.

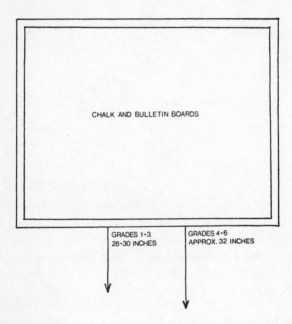

CHALK AND BULLETIN BOARDS

GRADES 1-3
28-30 INCHES

GRADES 4-6
APPROX. 32 INCHES

Bulletin Boards

Cork covered bulletin boards are very satisfactory because cork shows no pin holes. However, fiberboard is an inexpensive and adequate substitute. Fiberboard may be purchased at a building supply center. Rather than painting fiberboard, cover it with fabric, such as burlap. Two large bulletin boards, sized according to the wall space available, are adequate for an assembly or open department room. These boards should be from 4-12 feet (1.2-3.6 cm) long (the larger, the better) and from 3-4 feet (90-120 cm) high. Install in each class area a bulletin board from 2 ½ -3 feet (75-90 cm) high and from 3-4 feet (90-120 cm) long. If the room is used by other groups that desire bulletin board space, investigate reversible boards.

Specifications ■ *Grades 1 to 3:* The boards should be mounted approximately 28-30 inches (70-75 cm) above the floor.

Grades 4 to 6: The boards should be mounted approximately 32-inches (80-cm) above the floor.

IMPROVING AN EXISTING FACILITY

Your Equipment

Survey the furnishings in your classroom. If they are too small or too large, exchange furniture with another department so that all benefit. If this exchange is not feasible, ask a carpenter in your church to adjust chairs and tables to correct heights. Appropriately sized furnishings are important if the child is to be comfortable in his learning environment. Painting and repairing furnishings can be done with the combined efforts of parents and teachers.

Your Room

From the time a child enters your room on Sunday morning, the surroundings affect that child's attitude and resulting learning. The effect may be positive or negative. Bend down so you can see the room from the eye level of the child. As you look around the room objectively, consider these questions:

1. How do you feel about entering the room? Do you want to come in?
2. Is the room neat and clean? Does the air smell fresh?
3. Is the room colorful and light?
4. Is there something in the room that is particularly attractive to you?

5. Do you feel encouraged to become involved in an activity, or is everything so sterile you are reluctant to touch anything?

6. Are there windows you can easily see through?

7. Is there an activity you can do alone if you do not want to work with another person?

8. Can you choose a quiet activity or one that will involve movement?

9. Can you find and return the materials you need?

10. Is there space enough to move about without bumping into furniture?

11. Is the furniture and equipment useful and comfortable for the age group that will be using it? Does the furniture add or detract from the atmosphere in the room?

12. Are the bulletin boards and chalkboards at the eye level of the learners? Does the material displayed on them encourage Bible learning?

13. Are toilet facilities easily accessible?

14. Is there a drinking fountain nearby?

As you answer these questions, list (in order of priority) the things you want to change in your room. Determine which of the adjustments you can do with little or no help. Then accomplish these as money, time, materials and space become available. Work around those things you cannot change. However, begin developing long-range plans and strategies to insure that the more formidable projects will be accomplished at a future date.

If your church is in the process of building or remodeling an educational unit, be sure that the building committee includes some who are actively or recently involved in the educational program. At a teacher's meeting, discuss what needs and changes ought to be suggested to the building committee. Present those ideas to the building committee with specifications and suggestions; be prepared to share briefly sound, educationally-based reasons to validate your suggestions. Also, building committees need to be encouraged to build for growth so there will be no immediate need for additional space.

When space is at a premium, consider moving certain items

(such as adult-size chairs, lecterns, etc.) to give a feeling of openness. Is there another way in which the necessary furniture and equipment might be arranged to increase open space and flexibility? If you have a piano, can it be removed and an Autoharp, guitar or cassette player be used to accompany singing? Can some of the tables be removed? Many of the activities usually requiring a flat surface can be done on the floor. Younger children are often content to sit on a rug or carpeted area. Stop and think! Is it really necessary for every child to sit on a chair at any one time? If not, perhaps it will be possible to gain additional space by removing some of the chairs.

If the space available to you is adequate, think about rearranging furnishings and equipment to the greatest advantage. For example, placing bookcases back to back makes a low divider while creating separate work areas. Such items as book racks, coatrack, shelves (both closed and open), storage cabinets, paint racks and easels, chalkboards, and bulletin boards all need to be considered and placed around the room as valuable aids to learning (see Diagrams 1 and 2).

Make several diagrams of your classroom. First, sketch the room as it presently exists. Then have the department staff think of different arrangements that would meet the needs of your program. You will probably discover several alternatives. Then sketch on paper the arrangement that seems most effective before spending time and energy rearranging furniture.

Changes require organization and advanced planning so teachers know what to expect. A thoughtful rearrangement of facilities can bring about a healthy learning environment. You will want to find enough balance between change and routine so students can be flexible and still feel secure.

The Assembly Room with Small Classrooms

Your room may not be flexible enough to accommodate a variety of activities. For example, if your facility provides a large assembly room with small adjoining classrooms, consider removing some nonessential walls. Diagram 1 is an "open" room with nonessential walls removed. This open room has many possible uses, such as working areas for both small and large group activities. The materials children will need for activities may be prearranged so that little or no moving of equipment is needed during the Sunday School hour, except possibly moving chairs. This open room is flexible, not only for Sunday School, but also for a variety of uses during the week.

If the facility has several small classrooms surrounding an assembly area and no walls can be removed, this arrangement can still be very practical. Look at Diagram 2 for a possible arrangement to facilitate children's participating in a variety of learning activities. Note that doors have been removed (or left open) to encourage children to move easily from one area to another. Use one of the small rooms for a supply center. Blend together all rooms by painting walls and/or furniture complementary colors.

The Temporary Classroom

As building costs have soared in recent years, many churches have found it necessary to get multiple use out of many educational rooms. If your room is shared by other groups, or you are renting space for just one session per week, consider these ideas:

1. Storage of supplies is often a problem when a room is shared. If you cannot have your own locked cupboard in the room, secure sturdy cardboard file boxes in which to store supplies. If possible, store the carton in another room. If that's not possible, each teacher may need to carry his or her own carton back and forth each week.

2. Meet with the other users of your room to come to an agreement on the best arrangement of furniture and equipment in order to minimize custodial shifting of heavy objects. If possible, try to have the same age groups using the same rooms.

3. Work with other groups to establish policies for the use of the shared equipment. What can be placed on the walls or bulletin boards? When are the wastebaskets to be emptied? How

much cleanup must be done by teachers and what can the custodial staff be expected to do?

Refuse to be discouraged whatever your room and equipment situation. "I can do everything through him who gives me
strength" (Phil. 4:13). Pray earnestly for wisdom to accomplish
your plans. "For the LORD gives wisdom, and from his mouth
come knowledge and understanding" (Prov. 2:6).

RESOURCES

For additional suggestions to improve your children's classrooms, see:
Lowell E. Brown, *Sunday School Standards* (Ventura, CA: Gospel Light
Publications, Revised Edition, 1986), pp. 112-130.

Grading, Grouping and Growing

At times Jesus instructed large groups of people, but the majority of His teaching experiences were in small groups, including 57 recorded person-to-person encounters. In these small groups people learned of their needs and of the Savior's purposes, promises and plans for their lives.

The children in our Sunday Schools need consistent and personal encounters with adults who love the Lord and who are willing and prepared to express that love. This kind of interaction can occur when a group of six to eight children are permanently assigned to a teacher. Consider the advantages of working with children in such a ratio:

1. Small groups help students feel like they belong. Children are able to share with one another, and out of this interaction can come mutual understanding and acceptance.

2. In a small group, a teacher can easily learn each student's background, needs and interests. Such knowledge makes a teacher more effective in meeting individual needs.

3. Small groups allow students to participate fully, thereby encouraging maximum satisfaction.

4. Small groups provide a viable setting for evaluation of the learning progress.

5. Small groups are ideal for using creative methods, which allow each child to participate in (rather than simply observe) all steps of the learning process: listening, exploring, discovering, appropriating, and assuming responsibility (see chapter 7).

6. Small groups lessen the potential for behavior problems.

7. Small groups encourage numerical growth, because both members and visitors can be given the teacher's personal attention.

8. Small groups encourage a child's spiritual growth through a more personal relationship with the teacher.

GRADING—BASIS FOR GROWTH

Some Definitions

There are three basic groupings into which children can be organized for effective learning:

1. *Class.* A group of up to six or eight children, assigned to a teacher for Bible study.

The teacher accepts responsibility to develop significant relationships with these children and their parents. Whenever the size of a children's class exceeds six to eight, the quality of these relationships becomes difficult to establish and maintain. Also, direct involvement in learning becomes more difficult for each child, reducing learning efficiency and often increasing behavior problems.

2. *Department.* Two or more classes.

Just as class sizes should be carefully limited, so should that of departments. Four classes, providing for approximately 30 children, should be the maximum number for a children's department. This structure allows departments to effectively bring their classes together sometime during the Sunday School hour for a meaningful large group experience. This departmental arrangement also makes possible regular planning among the teachers of the department, an essential ingredient for consistent growth and improvement. Both the large group time and planning are enhanced when all classes in a department study the same lesson.

3. *Division.* Two or more departments for grades 1-6.

The departments within a division meet separately on Sunday morning, and may study different lesson material. The teachers within a division may meet periodically for training and general planning (see chapter 13 for specific job descriptions).

Kinds of Departments

Because childhood years are times of marked development in skills, comprehension and social interests, churches have long found that grouping children by school grade is an effective and desirable procedure.

Many Sunday Schools group children into a department for each grade level, e.g., a first grade department, a second grade department. These departments are termed *closely-graded.* Teachers plan together on a regular basis. All classes within a department come together for Bible Sharing (see chapter 11).

Churches also effectively group together children who are in different public school grade levels. When two grade levels are grouped together into a department, the department is called *dual-graded.* Since children develop at varying rates, there are usually some students from the younger grade who have advanced in some ways beyond some students in the older grade. Reading and writing skills are often the most obvious differences a teacher notices in a dual-graded setting.

While dual-grading may cause teachers to "stretch" procedures to fit the ability range of the group, the two-grade department is a very workable arrangement.

Because all classes study the same material, a dual-graded

AS YOUR CHILDREN'S DIVISION GROWS

● . . .divide your CLASSES as follows:

	8 students 1 class	**16** students 2 classes	**24** students 3 classes	**48** students 6 classes	**96** students 12 classes
G R A D E S	1 2 3 4 5 6	1 2 / 3 4 / 5 6	1 2 / 3 4 / 5 6	1 / 2 / 3 / 4 / 5 / 6	1 1 / 2 2 / 3 3 / 4 4 / 5 5 / 6 6

(Classes should not exceed 8 members at which time a new class should be formed.)

● . . .group your classes to form DEPARTMENTS as follows:

For Sunday Schools with 2 or more classes in 2-grade groups

G R A D E S	1	2
	1	2
	3	4
	3	4
	5	6
	5	6

For Sunday Schools which have 2 or more classes per grade

1	1	1
2	2	2
3	3	3
4	4	4
5	5	5
6	6	6

department benefits from teachers planning together. Also, when children come together for Bible Sharing, the Bible learning experiences of each class have relevance for the entire department.

Some Sunday Schools are forced by limited facilities or circumstances beyond their control to group together more than two grade levels of children. This structure, sometimes called a *tri-graded* or *multi-graded department,* requires the teacher to be very sensitive to the children's wide range of abilities; and then plan learning activities to accommodate that range. As a general rule, the wider the age span in a class or department, the greater the skill needed by teachers and leaders.

FACTORS IN GRADING AND GROUPING

For grading to contribute to the orderly growth of a Sunday School, three major factors need to be considered.

Attendance

The first factor to consider is the number of children attending your Sunday School. No more than 30 regularly-attending students should be assigned to a children's department. No more than six to eight children attending regularly should be assigned to each class within a department.

Available Space and Equipment

The second factor that influences the grading of children into manageable groups is the availability of space and equipment. After you determine the number of departments needed to care adequately for your children, take an inventory of the rooms now being used.

Your church may be allocating only two rooms for a children's department when four are needed. Whenever any part of the Sunday School needs additional space, the total Sunday School leadership needs to be involved in finding the best solution. Options include:

1. Exchanging rooms with other age groups.

2. Dividing space currently being used. Investigate possibility of adding or removing walls to accommodate this kind of change. Often, older buildings have been divided inefficiently. Changing partitions can sometimes create more useable space.

3. Secure new space through rental, purchase, construction or use of portable classrooms.

4. Reschedule parts of the program, providing double sessions of Sunday School.

If the available rooms will not adequately house departments with four full classes, you may need to limit the size of your departments to fit the rooms you have. Several small departments are better for children than one large, overcrowded one.

Available Leadership

The amount of leadership available and needed to staff the children's departments is of crucial importance. New classes can function adequately only when a sufficient teaching staff is provided.

Because a teacher is needed for each group of six to eight children in attendance, start planning for an additional teacher whenever the size of a class begins to near its limit. Also, begin planning to enlist a new department leader when an existing department begins to approach 30 children.

The first step in recruitment is to involve your total staff—leaders and teachers—in praying about the need for more people to get involved. Then compile a list of those who might be capable of becoming teachers. Contact these prospects in a personal, face-to-face way for best results. They should be fully informed of the importance of this ministry, of the duties involved in teaching, of how teaching is accomplished in the department and of the average time required to fill the role successfully.

Observation of an actual Sunday School session is essential to acquaint these individuals with teaching/learning procedures.

Training opportunities such as the department planning meetings should also be shared. Be certain to point out the spiritual growth resulting from teaching, for both the teacher and the students. Satisfactory departmental groupings, adequate space and equipment and a sufficient staff of dedicated workers are basic requirements for the orderly and effective growth of your children's ministry.

An Effective Teaching Schedule

"What a morning! I thought class time would never end!" a fourth grade teacher sighed as he left his room.

"We had quite a morning too," replied another teacher in the department. "We just can't get through all the lesson material during our class period."

Both teachers expressed frustration in terms of a time schedule. However, a closer look at what happened in each situation might lead us to conclude that the problem was not the length of the class time, but how each teacher used it. A successful teacher is continually alert for ways to use teaching time effectively. This chapter focuses on how to make the best use of time within the class session—and then how to use time efficiently in getting ready for the class session.

TOTAL SESSION TEACHING: What Is It?

Each part of your Sunday School morning schedule should contribute to the learning experiences of the child. Just as all the pieces of a puzzle interlock to produce one picture, so should every part of your session fit into a unified purpose. Total session teaching (1) focuses the entire session on a specific Bible truth and its application in daily living; (2) Non-lesson-related material is eliminated, thereby allowing maximum time for lesson-oriented learning; (3) The department leader and the teachers have definite goals and guidelines for their work in the various groupings within the department; (4) A total teaching session approach results in increased learning opportunities for the students because all information and experiences relate to one specific Bible truth.

A TOTAL TEACHING SESSION SCHEDULE

While there are many different ways to put a session together, the following plan has proven highly effective because it meets children where they are, provides variety within stability, and allows for ample reinforcement of the Bible truth without the boring sameness of mere repetition.

Basic Plan B

The old saying that "Sunday School begins when the first child arrives" continues to be valid, regardless of a child's age or the size of the Sunday School. Immediately upon arrival, the child goes to his or her permanent **Bible Study** group and becomes involved in one or more **Bible Readiness** choices. These simple activities start the child thinking about the biblical concepts that will be developed in the Bible lesson. Offering the child a choice gets the child involved in accepting personal responsibility to participate and learn. It also aids the teacher in meeting the varied needs within a group. For example, a nonreader may be more comfortable discovering information from pictures than from printed material.

    Bible Story is the second part of the **Bible Study** segment. During this time the teacher introduces the Bible story, weaving in opportunities for children to share (briefly) insights they gained from their **Bible Readiness** choices. **Bible Story** also becomes much more than listening to a story when learners become active participants by using their own Bibles to find the answers to questions the teacher asks. Even beginning readers can be led to locate names of Bible characters or key words in the Bible narrative. Advanced readers enjoy the challenge of discovering for themselves what the Bible really says.

The third part of the **Bible Study** segment is **Bible Application.** Here the teacher leads the children in discovering the relationship between Bible truths they have been studying and their day-to-day experiences. This experience is crucial to a child's learning! An exciting experience occurs when a child unlocks God's Word in terms of reality! Children also become familiar with the Bible memory verse during the **Bible Study** portion of the schedule.

This uninterrupted and unhurried (25-35 minutes) flow of Bible study at the beginning of the lesson when children are at their peak of learning efficiency increases significantly the amount and depth of Bible learning. The extra time for those children who arrive early is an added bonus.

When **Bible Study** is complete, each class immediately begins working on a **Bible Learning Activity.** Children need (and desire) opportunities to "be doers of the word, and not hearers only"! (See Jas. 1:22.) A well-balanced session provides children with the opportunity to apply Bible truths to everyday living in a variety of ways. The activities also involve a child in using the Bible to review and reinforce information and concepts, and/or to stimulate new learning.

A **Bible Learning Activity** may involve art, music, writing, drama or other skills. But always there is opportunity for Bible research at the child's level of ability. These activities may be completed in one session or extended over the entire unit of lessons, usually three to five Sundays. Unit-long activities can be more challenging and enjoyable than if all parts of a project had to be finished in one Sunday. However, varied attendance patterns may make one-Sunday activities more practical. Note: Bible Learning Activities differ from Bible Readiness Choices; Readiness Choices are brief activities (up to 5 minutes) intended to capture interest, while Bible Learning Activities are longer (about 20 minutes) and should bring about a sense of completion.

Bible Sharing/Worship is the last segment in a total teaching

BASIC PLAN B	TEACHER:	DEPARTMENT LEADER:
1. BIBLE STUDY (Early Time + 25-35 minutes) **Bible Readiness:** Activities to build readiness for Bible story. **Bible Story:** Presentation of visualized Bible story. **Bible Application:** Relationship of Bible truths to day-by-day experience.	Meets with permanent class group; Guides Bible Readiness; Leads Bible story; Helps children to apply Bible truths.	Greets visitors; Assigns new children to classes; Assists teachers as needed; Works with children with special needs; Observes class groups.
2. BIBLE LEARNING ACTIVITIES (20-25 minutes) Creative activities to reinforce Bible truths.	Guides children in creative Bible-related activities.	
3. BIBLE SHARING/WORSHIP (up to 15 minutes) **Includes:** Songs, offering, prayer and various worship activities related to unit focus and lesson aims. (On the fourth Sunday of each unit, allow additional time for children to share Bible Learning Activities from previous Sundays of the unit.)	Assists in leading worship; Sits with and worships with children. Option: Teacher may lead this segment for his or her class if no other classes study the same lesson.	Gives signal for large group time; Leads worship. Option: If classes study different courses, leader may follow plans for one of the courses each unit.

ALTERNATE PLAN A	Simply switches the order of Bible Learning Activities and Bible Sharing.

1. BIBLE STUDY (Early Time + 25-35 minutes)
2. BIBLE SHARIING/WORSHIP (15-20 minutes)
3. BIBLE LEARNING ACTIVITIES (20 minutes)

session. The department leader (or teacher) guides this time of songs, prayer, and varied worship activities related to the lesson/ unit aims. **Bible Sharing/Worship** builds on what each class has been learning. It involves children in sharing (in a variety of ways) what they have learned about the Bible story, Bible verse and life application.

If classes in the department study different lessons, the leader plans a balanced program that relates to common elements in the learning of each class, or each teacher may lead his or her class in Bible Sharing experiences.

Children may share their Bible Learning Activities on one Sunday of the unit. Different activity groups may share their activities different Sundays or all groups may share on the last Sunday of the unit. This sharing adds another effective means of reinforcing Bible learning.

Alternate Plan A

Another schedule involving the total teaching session approach is *Alternate Plan A.* This schedule can be used by any department with two to five classes all studying the same lesson. Plan A also makes **Bible Study (Bible Readiness, Bible Story** and **Bible Application)** the starting point for each session, providing a biblical foundation for all of the activities that follow during the session. The difference in this plan is that **Bible Sharing** (when all children and teachers in the department come together) occurs in the middle of the hour rather than at the end.

Plan A allows children to choose **Bible Learning Activities** at the end of Bible Sharing on the first Sunday of each unit. Each teacher in the department guides one Bible Learning Activity. Each child selects a Bible Learning Activity, not necessarily the one his permanent Bible Study class teacher is guiding. For example, one teacher might be prepared to lead an art activity and another teacher to lead a group in music. The leader briefly explains both activities to the group, but does not tell which teacher will lead each activity. This procedure helps assure that the child chooses the activity of highest personal interest.

Not all children always get their first choice, as group sizes must be limited. However, the process of choosing greatly increases interest; and as a result learning improves. If children will work on one activity for the entire unit, children choose activities on the first Sunday of each unit. The activity group works together for the remaining Sundays of the unit, sharing their accomplishments on the last Sunday. If you offer one-Sunday activities, children choose an activity each week.

Notice that the diagram also outlines specifically the responsibilities of the teachers and department leaders during each segment of the schedule.

What are the advantages of using Plan A? Moving from small class groups in the middle of the session to join another group helps children stay alert. It is helpful for children to work closely with more than one teacher. Because children work with the same teacher every Sunday in the Bible Study segment of the schedule, that important relationship is maintained. Also, Plan A allows children a choice of Bible Learning Activities.

Plan B suggests children change groups only once. They remain in their permanent class for both Bible Study and Bible Learning Activities, then move to the Bible Sharing/Worship group.

The similarities between the two plans are more striking than the differences. Both plans provide for a total teaching session approach. Both plans offer exactly the same major time segments that add up to efficient use of time on Sunday mornings. Both allow activities to be planned for each session or to continue over the entire unit of study. Grouping lessons into units increases learning while actually saving teacher preparation time.

Both plans allow significant time for building strong teacher/child relationships. At the same time the plans provide ample time for activities that make children active participants in Bible learning experiences rather than passive spectators.

As you review Plans A and B, evaluate your teaching situation. Do you provide for all segments of the suggested plan during your session? Is the balance of small and large group time appropriate? Could you use time more efficiently?

The boldfaced titles for the parts of the session are taken from Gospel Light's Children's Division curriculum. You may use other terminology, but these lesson segments are each vital elements of a solid Bible learning session.

HOW TO CHOOSE THE BEST PLAN FOR YOU

Use **Basic Plan B** if . . .

■ your department has less than one hour available (omit Bible Sharing/Worship);

■ two (or more) courses are taught;

■ less than ten children (or more than 30) are in attendance.

Use **Alternate Plan A** if . . .

■ two or more classes study the same course (classes may be same or different grade levels);

■ classes are located in or adjacent to department room;

■ teachers plan together regularly.

HOW TO GET STARTED

Start using Plan B schedule by introducing only one new step at a time. For example, you might start by using one or two Bible Readiness choices as the children arrive. It will be helpful if one of them is an independent activity—one in which children can work on their own without your direct help (e.g., a Bible learning game children are already familiar with).

Help children learn to work independently (a) by providing written instructions on stand-up cards made from parts of file folders or large index cards or by providing instructions on a cassette tape; (b) by having all supplies available; (c) by storing in a special place Bible learning games that children may choose as they complete other activities.

When you and the children are comfortable using the Bible

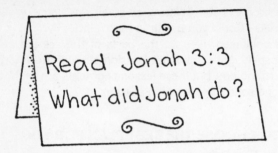

Readiness choices at the beginning of your class time, start using a Bible Learning Activity toward the end of your class time. You or your children choose which activity to work on.

When you and the children are comfortable using Bible Learning Activities in class time, consider the possibility of letting children choose Bible Learning Activity groups as suggested in Plan A. If you follow Plan A, change your schedule to include the three blocks of time suggested in the diagram.

IF YOU HAVE MORE THAN 60 MINUTES

Many churches have extended their Sunday School schedule to a 75-minute block of time. They increase by five minutes each of the three main segments of the hour.

IF YOU HAVE LESS THAN 60 MINUTES

Trying to shorten any of the main time segments in Plan A or Plan B usually results in harried teachers and frustrated children. In most situations with limited time, it is best to eliminate one time block completely. The Bible Study time block should always be retained. If most of your children will participate in worship experiences in Churchtime, consider eliminating Bible Sharing/Worship. If you decide to eliminate Bible Learning Activities, plan to give a little more time for participation in Bible Readiness choices.

IF YOU ARE RESPONSIBLE FOR CHURCHTIME

If you are working with a *total morning* program (including both the Sunday School and Churchtime) the following schedule provides for up to a one-and-a-half hour Churchtime (or extended session) following the dismissal of Sunday School.

Get Together Time (15-20 minutes) • This informal time of games, fun songs and refreshments helps to meet the physical and social needs of children.

Bible Discovery Time (20-30 minutes) • Children discover Bible information in a variety of ways (art, drama, games, music, etc.)

Praise Time (20-30 minutes) • Use music, Bible verses, present-day situations related to Bible truths; prayer, provide a worship experience at the child's level of understanding.

Wrap Up Time (5-15 minutes) • Bible games, puzzles and books provide Bible-related activities for children to conclude the morning (optional).

The terminology in this suggested schedule indicates specific parts of the Churchtime programs published by Gospel Light Publications. Regardless of the terminology, the schedule segments are vital elements of an extended session for children.

Productive Lesson Planning

Up to now we have focused on the use of time within the class session. Of equal importance is the use of time during the week in getting ready for the class session. The teacher who makes wise use of limited time will be able to walk into the classroom feeling confident, while the teacher who is unwise in preparation will either feel inadequate because of too little preparation or burdened by having spent more time than is really necessary.

INDIVIDUAL LESSON PLANNING

Most teachers prepare their lessons individually. This method has the advantage of allowing a person to work at his or her own pace, doing the preparation at the most convenient time and place.

Consider the following tips for effective preparation. The Lesson Plan Sheet at the end of this chapter is a helpful tool to use in guiding preparation.

1. Preview a unit of lessons before starting work on any individual lessons. Having an idea of where the next month of study is leading will make your preparation more efficient and purposeful.

2. Read the Bible passages and aims early in the week in order to allow Scripture to speak to your own life. Pray that the

Holy Spirit will enable you to grow through considering each passage.

3. Identify one main truth you want your children to remember and apply. Make this the focus of all you do in the session.

4. Outline your Bible story. Identify any visuals you will use, questions you will ask, and times during the story when you will ask children to use their own Bibles.

5. Plan the Bible Learning Activities you will provide to involve your children in exploring and applying Scripture:

a. Identify and collect all necessary materials.

b. Write out clear instructions you will use to lead children in completing each activity. (Writing directions is the best way to check that your directions are not confusing.)

c. Write out several questions or statements to use as children are working on the activity. Your conversation is crucial to helping an activity accomplish real Bible learning.

Individual preparation also has a few limitations: Some teachers are not well enough disciplined to set aside adequate time for proper preparation; teachers who prepare alone do not receive the benefit of ideas and suggestions from others who teach the same materials; teachers who prepare alone are less likely to try something new to improve teaching skills than are those who prepare with other teachers. Read the next section of this chapter for help in how to plan with at least one other teacher in your department.

DEPARTMENTAL LESSON PLANNING

The apostle Paul often wrote to the early Christians urging them to work in a spirit of cooperation rather than independence—in a spirit of "we" rather than "I." "Each of you should look not only to your own interests, but also to the interests of others" (Phil. 2:4). "From him [Christ] the whole body, joined and held together by every supporting ligament, grows and builds itself up in love, as each part does its work" (Eph. 4:16).

In no area of your church is the biblical pattern for working together more essential than in a Children's Department. Leadership of the department should not work in isolation. Each part of the Sunday morning program, including the Churchtime program, must be knit together by the leaders and teachers planning together. The department leader, as the title implies, has the initial responsibility for putting the apostle Paul's words of admonition into action.

Note: In many cases, a department leader may not feel competent to lead teachers in the planning process. When this occurs, two or more departments may join together for all or part of the meeting. The person chosen to lead such a session should be capable of encouraging and instructing department leaders to help them grow in their leadership role. See chapter 13 for ways a teaching staff may function effectively.

PLANNING MEETINGS

For children to have effective Bible learning experiences, the staff needs to think and plan together regularly. The staff that sets aside time to meet as a group will find their individual preparation efforts are simplified and made more productive.

Effective Sunday School workers have long recognized the need for a well-coordinated team effort in each department. Even though an individual teacher may do admirable work independent of others on the staff, the total impact of such effort is much less than when it is part of a cooperative venture.

Perhaps more than curriculum resources, classroom supplies, furniture or equipment, Sunday School teachers need other teachers. Teachers need the stimulation and support that can only come from someone who shares similar challenges.

Schedule departmental planning meetings at least once a month before the beginning of the unit. Staff members, including department leader, teachers and secretary need to be part of the meeting. Each meeting should be conducted by the department leader, or an appropriate leader of the Sunday School.

Basic Tasks of a Department Planning Meeting

If you have a small number of teachers, or if a department leader does not feel competent to lead each of these segments of a Planning Meeting, items 1 and 2 can be done with teachers from two or more departments—even the whole Sunday School— meeting together, and led by the division coordinator, general superintendent or other leader of the Sunday School. Item 3 can be done with as few as two teachers or in a large group with a skilled leader.

1. Ministry to Each Other ■ For staff members to function together in an effective and happy manner, they need to know one another personally. Planning meetings can become settings for personal interaction—times when all staff members may share their interests, concerns and joys. Building up one another in Christ can encourage personal spiritual growth for each staff member. For example, form prayer partners by asking each staff member to write his or her name and an item of concern on a slip of paper. Each person draws a slip and prays daily for the person whose name they drew. At the next meeting, share evidences of God's answers to prayer. And thank Him for His goodness! Then exchange new slips.

Studying God's Word together is another opportunity to encourage the spiritual growth of staff members. Before trying to teach children what God's Word says, it is essential to examine the Scriptures to discover personally God's truth. Teachers can help each other find meaningful insights in the passages children will be taught in coming weeks.

2. Skill Improvement ■ For teachers to grow in their ability to guide children effectively, planning meetings must include a teacher education feature, such as ways to use creative Bible teaching methods, interpreting age-level characteristics, etc. Poll staff members to determine which topics are of greatest interest.

The department leader's Sunday morning observations will help in discovering areas in which teachers need help.

For training to be effective, the leader must present the material in light of the next few lessons to be taught. It does little good for a teacher to be told of exciting new teaching methods unless time is spent demonstrating and practicing those methods as part of an upcoming lesson.

3. Unit/Lesson Planning ■ Before planning the coming unit of lessons, evaluate the current unit. What worked? What did not? What should be changed? What responses from students can help teachers determine if the Bible Teaching/Learning Aims were accomplished?

UNIT PLANNING

Curriculum materials arranged into units (three to five lessons, all with a similar purpose) simplify teachers' planning. Grouping lessons into units helps teachers think of each unit more as one continuing lesson rather than as a series of isolated lessons. At the planning meeting, the leader distributes unit and lesson plan sheets to teachers. Churchtime staff uses Churchtime planning sheets. (See planning sheet samples in this chapter.) Teachers complete planning sheets as meeting progresses. The leader guides teachers to become familiar with:

- Unit aims and Scripture on which Bible study is based
- Bible memory verses
- Songs suggested for the unit
- Bible Learning Activities suggested for the unit.

LESSON PLANNING

Then leader and teachers plan in detail the first lesson of the unit. For example, teachers discuss and select Bible Readiness choices. One teacher, previously assigned by leader, demonstrates use of Bible story visuals; another teacher shows a completed *Student Guide* page. Each teacher selects a Bible Learning Activity for which he or she will be responsible during each Sunday of the unit. As teachers discuss and select Bible learning experiences, the leader helps teachers know how each activity helps to accomplish the Bible Teaching/Learning Aim. The meeting concludes with announcements pertaining to the department. Group dismisses with prayer.

MULTI-LESSON DEPARTMENT PLANNING MEETING

Even teachers who use different lesson materials will find value in meeting together regularly. These meetings can encourage a teacher's spiritual and personal growth as well as improving teaching technique. The first two items listed as "Basic Tasks for a Department Planning Meeting" (in this chapter) are applicable for a multi-lesson department planning meeting.

Teachers can also benefit from sharing information about planning procedures. For example, ask a teacher to demonstrate the step-by-step methods he or she uses to plan a unit of lessons. This model then serves as a guide for teachers to use in their individual planning. Some departments have teachers plan individually as part of the meeting, then join together for questions and discussion.

A portion of each meeting can also be used profitably to make Bible games (see Resources at the conclusion of this chapter), learn new songs, organize picture file, etc.

TIPS FOR DEPARTMENT PLANNING MEETINGS

■ **Set meeting date well in advance.** Establish a regular day of the month, or week, for Sunday School Planning Meetings.

■ **Notify teachers well in advance in person.** Teachers are busy people and often cannot rearrange schedules to accommodate a hastily announced meeting.

■ **Give preparation assignments.** When teachers come prepared, the meeting will accomplish a great deal more than if everyone simply arrives. Also, assignments increase each participant's sense of responsibility to attend. (See Step 4 under "A Planning Meeting Guide" for possible assignments.)

■ **Remind teachers of meeting.** The Sunday before the meeting is a good time to personally remind each teacher of the meeting time and location.

■ **Assist teachers with possible problems.** If transportation and baby-sitting are two common problems that interfere with attendance, develop a plan to deal with them.

■ **Prepare a realistic agenda for the meeting.** (See "A Planning Meeting Guide" below.)

■ **Eliminate factors that might deter meeting from the purpose of planning and training.** For example, redoing bulletin boards or cleaning supply shelves are secondary to the Sunday School's purpose of teaching the Bible. Such tasks should not be allowed to take up valuable planning and training time. Set a separate date to accomplish these maintenance tasks.

See charts on following pages.

A PLANNING MEETING GUIDE
Use this guide for each of the three unit planning meetings in each quarter.

BEFORE

Department Leader:	**All Staff:**
• Schedules meeting	• Read Bible Overview, Bible Learning Activities and unit of lessons.
• Makes assignments for first lesson of unit—	• Complete assignments.
a teacher to complete Bible Readiness choices;	
a teacher to complete Bible story visuals from *Teaching Resources*;	
a teacher to complete a sample of *Student Guide* sheet.	

DURING

1. Leader summarizes unit Bible content and leads staff in brief discussion. Volunteer prays for needs of staff and children.
2. All read Unit Focus, Value and Bible Skill.
3. Learn Unit Songs by listening, then singing along.
*4. For first lesson of each unit:
   Leader summarizes Bible Teaching/Learning Aims and reads Bible Verse to Know
   Teacher demonstrates the Bible Readiness choices
   Each teacher decides the choices to offer his or her class
   Teacher demonstrates use of Bible story visuals
   Teacher shows complete *Student Guide* sheet.
5. Leader describes Unit Bible Learning Activities. Each teacher selects one Bible Learning Activity to prepare and guide.
6. Discuss visitor and absentee followup.
7. Discuss announcements and information pertaining to your department.

* If you have a weekly planning meeting, follow this procedure for planning each lesson.

LESSON PLAN SHEET—Grades 1-6

Lesson Title: _____ Date: _____

Read Lesson Focus, Bible Verse to Know, Lesson Aims from *Teacher's Manual.*

1. **BIBLE STUDY** (25-35 minutes)
   a. Bible Readiness
   My Activities:

   Materials:

   Conversation/Questions:

   b. Bible Story
   Outline of Bible Story:

   Materials:

   Conversation/Questions:

   c. Bible Application
   Student Worksheet Conversation/Questions:

2. **BIBLE LEARNING ACTIVITIES** (20-25 minutes)
   My Activity:

   Materials:

   Procedure:

   Conversation:

3. **BIBLE SHARING/WORSHIP** (up to 15 minutes)
   Materials:

   Order of Activities:

CHURCHTIME PLAN SHEET—Grades 1-6

Lesson Title: _____ Date: _____
Read the Session Focus/Session Goal from Leader's Manual.

1. **GET TOGETHER TIME** (15-20 minutes)
   A large group time of games and refreshments.
   Games:

   Refreshments:

2. **BIBLE DISCOVERY TIME** (20-30 minutes)
   A small group time of Bible learning.
   My Activity:

   Materials:

   Procedure:

   Conversation/Questions:

3. **PRAISE TIME** (20-30 minutes)
   A large group time of worship and fellowship.
   Materials:

   Order of Activities:

4. **WRAP-UP TIME** (5-15 minutes)
   A large and/or small group time of games, puzzles, etc.
   Activities/Materials:

RESOURCES

For ideas to use in building Bible Readiness or as Bible Learning Activities, see:

Barbara J. Bolton, *How to Do Bible Learning Activities: Grades 1-6, Book 1* (Ventura, CA: Gospel Light Publications, 1982).

Barbara J. Bolton, *How to Do Bible Learning Activities: Grades 1-6, Book 2* (Ventura, CA: Gospel Light Publications, 1984).

For help in planning and conducting effective department planning meetings, see:

Teacher Training Manual (Ventura, CA: Gospel Light Publications, Revised Edition, 1987).

Training Paks. ICL/Gospel Light has produced a wide variety of packets for use in individual departmental and divisional training, as well as with teachers of all ages meeting together. Contact your church supplier for a current listing.

Who Makes It Happen?

"Now you are the body of Christ,
    and each one of you is a part of it.
And in the church God has appointed
    first of all apostles,
        second prophets,
            third teachers."
            (1 Cor. 12:27,28)

"But to each one of us
    grace has been given as Christ apportioned it . . .
It was he who gave some to be apostles,
    some to be prophets,
        some to be evangelists,
            and some to be pastors and teachers."
            (Eph. 4:7,11)

The Lord Jesus gives gifts to those people whom He chooses for
His Body, the Church. One of the most reassuring aspects of
doing the Lord's work is the assistance He provides to those who
follow Him: "I labor, struggling with all his energy, which so powerfully works in me" (Col.1:29). We are co-workers with Christ!
God's own Spirit supplies the guidance, sensitivity and insight so
crucial to a successful ministry.

JOB DESCRIPTIONS

What are the specific tasks that need to be done to build a strong Christian education ministry? And who are the people who should be responsible to carry out those tasks?

The Teacher

There may be no higher calling in life than that of teacher. Repeatedly, in the Gospels, Jesus was addressed as "Teacher," a title showing respect and honor for Him as a person and for the vital role teachers play in the lives of people.

A teacher is called of God to personalize His Word in the lives of the learners. A teacher is in a real and vital partnership with the Holy Spirit to present the love of God to children.

Guiding and Encouraging ■ Every teacher needs a class small enough to allow personal guidance of each learner's spiritual growth. Bible study and learning activities are most effective in a small class group because of the crucial need for frequent teacher-child interaction. A small class also makes sustaining a child's interest easier for both child and teacher. A permanently assigned class of no more than six to eight children allows a teacher to build a personal relationship with each child.

The teacher's prime responsibility is to lead children in the study of God's Word through lesson-related Bible learning experiences. (See chapter 11 for every-Sunday details.) In order for the teacher to lead students into an understanding of the Lord Jesus and the meaning of being a member of God's family, the teacher must be building relationships with each child—and with the child's parents. Teacher-parent interaction provide mutual assistance to insure the best possible Bible learning experiences for the child at church and at home.

Cooperation and Planning ■ Only a teacher who continues to learn will be able to stimulate children in their learning. Therefore, time to study and improve teaching skills must be regularly set aside, even though a busy schedule will make preparation time difficult to protect. If Jesus, the Master Teacher, regularly retreated to find time alone for prayer and thought, how much more is it necessary for those who seek to follow His example? One of the best ways to make the most of limited preparation time is to meet regularly, at least once a month, with other teachers to pray and plan and encourage one another.

As a class grows, additional teachers are needed to maintain group sizes of no more than six to eight children per teacher.

As a department grows, the following staff positions take on specific teacher support functions, enabling the teachers to focus their efforts, while involving more people in significant areas of ministry.

Department Leader

When a department has three or more teachers, it is time to appoint a Department Leader.

The Department Leader is the lead teacher in the department. The leader oversees the entire program within one department and is alert to the way the program is being conducted. He or she may guide the Bible Sharing/Worship time each Sunday (see chapter 11). As an experienced teacher, the leader is able to suggest changes tactfully, encourage teachers, share resources and methods.

The Department Leader is a listener. Teachers need to know their suggestions and problems are being heard! The leader evaluates teaching skills; encourages teachers in areas of strengths and makes suggestions for improvements. Helping teachers to fulfill their assignments also means having the necessary equipment and materials available.

Recruitment and Training ■ The Department Leader needs to be alert to discover and bring potential leaders and teachers to the attention of the Sunday School administration. He or she must work closely with new teachers and train them by modeling effective teaching techniques. The leader should participate with the teachers in training classes, conventions and workshops.

Communication and Cooperation ■ The Department Leader

is the communicator between the teachers in his department and the Sunday School administration. The Department Leader is also concerned with establishing and maintaining communication with parents. Working closely with the children's families reinforces the impact of the Sunday School and facilitates the relationship between the learner and teacher.

Because the Department Leader is a "teacher of teachers," he or she needs to encourage teachers with words of praise, show empathy for their problems, and offer positive and practical ways to increase their teaching effectiveness. This kind of ministry involves becoming personally interested in each staff member, much as those staff members are expected to become interested in each child. The leader prays daily for each staff member by name. Also, the leader phones teachers each week to keep in touch.

Evaluation and Planning ■ Monthly, or more frequent, planning meetings are the responsibility of the Department Leader. Goals, challenges, teaching techniques and lesson planning should be discussed at the meetings. There is no substitute for these times of planning, sharing and praying together!

The Department Leader also works with the Outreach Leader to prepare for outreach and the new classes that outreach will necessitate. With the other members of the department, the leader must consider how to maintain the teacher-pupil ratio and plan for equipment and space needs.

Outreach Leader

A generation ago, most children's Sunday School teachers were housewives, able and willing to give five or more hours a week to lesson preparation, room decoration, class activities, absentee contacts, visitor follow-up and prospect cultivation.

As more and more women have taken on full- and part-time jobs outside the home, fewer teachers have continued doing these important tasks. In most cases, the first actions to be dropped were prospect cultivation. Visitor and absentee follow-up has also been seriously neglected. As a result, the past several decades have seen a significant decline in Sunday School outreach efforts—and a resulting decline in Sunday School and church growth.

Many churches have found that enlisting an Outreach Leader for every department is a very effective means of reversing the trend and renewing the Sunday School's commitment to reach out. An Outreach Leader actively seeks to locate prospects and makes the initial contact with each prospect. The Outreach Leader coordinates additional contacts as necessary, involving other staff members when possible. The Outreach Leader also works with the teachers to make sure all visitors are followed up, and keeps the staff informed about absentees who need personal attention.

Once a visitor is enrolled, the teacher is given the responsibility for building and maintaining contact with that child and family, but the Outreach Leader reminds, encourages and assists as necessary to ensure that teachers are able to stay on top of this crucial function.

Secretary

Consistent and accurate record-keeping produces information essential for maintaining a well-run department as well as planning for orderly growth. Statistics reflecting a child's birth date, attendance patterns, home address, grade level, church membership and family details provide valuable data on which to make decisions involving grouping, grading, follow-up, evangelism planning, outreach, etc.

As a department grows to around twenty, a secretary becomes highly beneficial to assist the Department Leader. Very often, the department secretary will be the first person the children see upon their arrival. A friendly and personal greeting makes a child's initial experience each Sunday a pleasant one. The secretary also assists teacher with supplies—and occasionally with a helping hand when a group is too large or an activity too challenging.

Maintenance of Records ■ The secretary accurately records attendance, offering details and registration information in cooperation with the Outreach Leader. Based on attendance data, the secretary orders necessary curriculum materials each quarter—and carefully labels and stores unused materials from previous quarters. In cooperation with the department leader, the secretary also enrolls and assigns new students to their classes.

Loving Person (Optional)

Not often do you find "loving person" listed as one of the staff members for a children's Christian education ministry! However, a person who is assigned this job, and who looks for opportunities each session to live up to that name, can be the key to a successful learning experience for the children within the department. For example, when a child exhibits need for special attention, the Loving Person is able to help the class and teacher by guiding that child in a one-to-one relationship. An accepting and loving attitude toward a child is shown by sitting with the child and helping him or her function attentively and productively. This assistance allows the teacher and other learners to continue without disruption. By attendance at each class session and focusing on the child with special needs, the Loving Person is demonstrating God's love in a way children can understand. Younger departments, those that are overcrowded, and those with one or more "difficult" children, tend to benefit most from adding a Loving Person to the staff.

DEPARTMENT DIAGRAM 1
(Fewer than 12 Children)

Children

DEPARTMENT DIAGRAM 2
(12-18 Children)

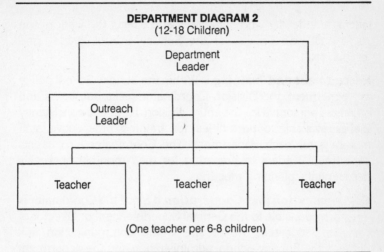

(One teacher per 6-8 children)

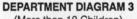

DEPARTMENT DIAGRAM 3
(More than 18 Children)

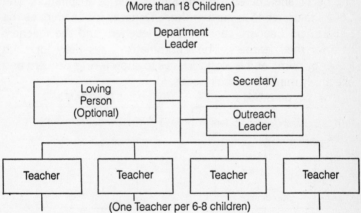

(One Teacher per 6-8 children)

Division Coordinator

When there are three or more departments within grades one through six (see chapter 10 for grouping and grading details) a Division Coordinator should be appointed. This person is responsible to the General Superintendent or the Director of Christian Education. The Division Coordinator is an experienced teacher and leader who supervises and directs the work of the entire children's division of the Sunday School, grades one through six.

Recruitment and Training ▪ Within the Sunday School policy for recruitment, the Division Coordinator seeks out, trains and organizes personnel for the entire division. He or she consistently makes available opportunities for training prospective staff members for each department. The Coordinator also assists department leaders in preparing for their monthly or weekly departmental planning meetings.

Communication and Cooperation ▪ Since the Coordinator is directly responsible to the General Superintendent or Director of Christian Education, he or she is the communication link between the Sunday School administration and the department leaders. At regularly scheduled meetings with department leaders, he or she shares information as well as inspiration. The Coordinator needs to nurture those Department Leaders as the Department Leaders care for their teachers and the teachers care for their learners. The Coordinator prays daily for each leader by name and is alert for ways to show loving concern and effectively minister to their needs.

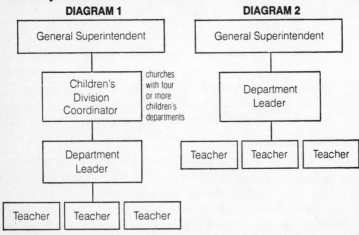

The Coordinator represents the children's division at Sunday School council (board, committee) meetings. He or she also works with the Outreach Leaders to plan for outreach efforts.

Evaluation and Planning ■ The Division Coordinator is continually envisioning the space and equipment necessary for growth. The Coordinator makes recommendations to the general superintendent to develop and maintain departments and classes of the proper size and to control the teacher-student ratio by creating new departments and classes. Planning regularly with department leaders is vital to insure cooperation and facilitate orderly and consistent growth.

Firsthand observation of each department, at least once per quarter, is essential for evaluation purposes. (Alerting department leaders ahead of time prevents their being surprised.) The Coordinator shares the evaluation personally with each Department Leader, pointing out strengths more than opportunities for improvement.

TEACHER/STUDENT RATIOS

The number of staff members needed depends on the number of people involved in a Sunday School. Just as experience has shown that one teacher is needed for every six to eight children, one leader is needed for every five people being supervised. For example, one Department Leader supervises two to five class teachers; one coordinator supervises two to five department leaders. A general superintendent supervises no more than five coordinators, department leaders or teachers. One of the best ways to accomplish the aims and objectives of your Sunday School is to establish and maintain this workable and productive staff member ratio.

The most common response to these ratios is a protest that it is almost impossible to enlist enough people to maintain a staff with significantly fewer people. This reply may be very true, but it overlooks one of the main causes of the difficulty churches face in enlisting teachers and leaders: most churches pile too much work on too few people. The plan outlined in this chapter has proven successful because it recognizes that no one person has been called to do everything; but everyone has been called to do something. This principle impacts a church's success in recruiting not only in the amount of work a person should be expected to do, but also in recognizing that most people do not have a wide variety of either natural talents or spiritual gifts. For example, there are people in any congregation who feel inadequate to teach, but who would be thrilled with the opportunity to serve as a Secretary, a Loving Person, or an Outreach Leader. Plus, the more people who become involved, the more other people will hear of the joys of serving Christ in children's ministries!

RESOURCES

For further help in developing effective job descriptions for your staff, see:
Lowell E. Brown, *Sunday School Standards* (Ventura, CA: Gospel Light Publications, Revised Edition, 1986), pp. 68,69,134.

For help in developing a training program for your staff, see:
Teacher Training Manual (Ventura, CA: Gospel Light Publications, Revised Edition, 1987).

PART 3

Skills and Tips for Better Teaching

How to Make Bible Stories Come Alive

Jesus is considered the master teacher, and much of His reputation as such results from the stories He told. The teacher who wants to communicate biblical truth must also become gifted in telling stories, for stories can make truth come alive in ways that children will long remember. While a picture may be worth a thousand words, a good story is worth a host of explanations.

Experiencing the Christian life is not simply a matter of adhering to statements of truth; the Christian life is a personal relationship with Christ most powerfully communicated through the examples of real people and their victories and struggles. Scripture narratives are the richest source of these examples.

Storytelling scares more new teachers than perhaps any other facet of teaching. The prospect of being responsible to capture the interest of squirming children and then to sustain that interest for the duration of a story, seems like more of a challenge than many people are ready to face. One of the most common responses people give when asked to teach children is: "Well, I could help, but don't ask me to tell the story."

Storytelling is a big hurdle for many people and for a wide variety of reasons:

■ Some find it hard to remember a story well enough to tell it effectively.

■ Some are nervous about speaking in front of a group.

■ Some worry about what to do if:
—a child misbehaves
—a child asks a question
—the group becomes bored
—the group has heard the story before.

■ Some worry about children's difficulty in understanding some aspects of a story.

■ Some are uncertain they can fill the time designated for the story.

Fortunately, effective storytelling is a skill that anyone can develop with practice by following a few simple principles:

1. Prepare and Practice Your Story

The mistakes people make in trying to tell a story can all be corrected with a little preliminary planning and practice. Everyone has had the experience of listening to someone who is trying to rethink what really happened. The storyteller may ramble, add too many insignificant details, leave out significant parts, or worst of all, drive everyone to frustration while trying to remember something that turns out to have absolutely no bearing on the story itself.

A little forethought can make all the difference between a story the audience wishes would end and the one the audience wishes would continue. Four essential steps should be taken in getting ready to tell any story:

■ Identify where the story is going. If you are clear about the purposes of the story, you will be less likely to wander off the track. Your curriculum provides a focus statement to help you identify the story's main point.

■ Outline the story, identifying the major events that occur.

■ Review the story facts enough so that each point in your outline will remind you of the details involved in that event.

■ Practice telling the story aloud using your outline to prompt you from one main point to the next. Tell your story to someone in your family, your pet, to a tape recorder or to yourself in the mirror.

2. Have Confidence in Your Story

Why is this story worth hearing? Ask yourself this question to be sure you are clear on the value of the story to your class. People will listen to a story that offers them a benefit.

What is the most interesting thing about this story? Ask yourself: What are the features of this story that compel attention? What will my class be drawn to as they listen?

A few moments spent answering these questions can help you build confidence in the value and the appeal of your story. When a storyteller is confident that the story has value and appeal, then he or she will be less concerned about storytelling ability.

Occasionally, every teacher comes across a story that for some reasons does not appear to "click." The teacher may not see how the story relates to the needs or interests of the class, or there may not be any factors in the story that give it strong appeal to the group. If the teacher is not at liberty to select a different story, it may be necessary to give this story a unique treatment to arouse interest. For example, one teacher felt the story of Jonathan giving his armor to David had little to interest her class of 5th grade girls. She decided to emphasize the covenant between friends and led them to compare this friendship with the relationship of Ruth and Naomi. In most cases, a beginning teacher should accept the fact that the stories in the curriculum have been chosen for good reason by people who understand the age level being taught.

3. Capture Interest at the Start

A good beginning is essential, because it is much easier to capture an audience than it is to recapture them after their attention has wandered. The surest way to kill interest is to ask, "Does anybody remember last week's story?" Nobody ever remembers last week's story except the teacher, who only remembers it because of having reviewed it the night before. If this week's story connects in any way to last week's story, you can jog your children's memories as you proceed.

The best way to begin most stories with children is through some type of experience of interest to everyone in the group. This experience needs to connect to some aspect of the story. Since most Bible stories are about people with strange sounding names who lived in faraway lands in a totally different culture, children need help to see how the story relates to something familiar. The younger your children, the more crucial it is to start a story with a reference to something in their own experience.

There are many ways in which to connect your story to the interests and experiences of your group:

■ Ask a question about something you know your children have seen or done. For example, to introduce the story of the wise men who followed the star, ask children to briefly tell of a time they looked up into a nighttime sky. Or, ask them about the longest journey they ever took. Or, invite them to tell about a favorite present they received. Share your own answer to the question to give children some insights into your life.

■ Share a *brief* illustration to introduce your story. This could be an incident from your own experience, something recently reported in the news, or something you have read. Just be sure the illustration deals with an area you know is interesting to your class and leads into your Bible story. It must be brief! A long introduction may capture interest, but it will use up some of the limited attention span of your group.

■ Involve your group in a readiness activity that prepares them for the story (see chapter 11):

• A game that reviews information taught in previous weeks can help bring those who were present as well as absentees to a similar level of information about events preceding today's story.

• Sketching a picture of a typical problem situation can

get children thinking about the problem faced by a person in the story.

• Comparing distances on a Bible map with those on a local area map can help children understand the time and effort involved by the people in today's story.

• Listening to a tape of a song can introduce children to concepts that are illustrated in the story.

• A sensory (touching, testing, etc.) experience can arouse interest and appreciation for some facet of the story you are going to tell.

4. Identify Children's Level of Familiarity with Story

Teachers face two opposing challenges in telling Bible stories to most groups of children. On one hand, there may be aspects of the story that are totally unfamiliar to children in your group. Customs, terminology, objects, relationships can all cause misunderstanding and confusion if not clearly explained.

On the other hand, some children have heard many of the Bible stories and may express boredom at the prospect of hearing "that old story again." An effective teacher keeps both these factors in mind in planning how to present a Bible story.

First, identify any aspects of your story you feel may be unfamiliar to at least some children in your group. It is usually easier to deal with these before actually launching the story narrative, rather than interrupting the flow of the story to stop and make an explanation.

For example, many Bible stories involve a well, but few children today have ever seen one, other than perhaps a "wishing well" at a park. Before telling a story involving a well, you might ask the class, "When you want a drink of water, where are some places you might get it? Where do you find water to wash your hands?" These questions allow those with little or no Bible background to answer easily. Next, ask, "Where do you think Bible time people went to get the water they needed?" A few more questions will give you a good idea of how much your children know about a well, and will give those with some Bible knowledge a chance to share their information. You can add any needed facts, and explain that knowing about a well is important for understanding today's Bible story.

Next, recognize that at least some members of the group have heard the story before. To remove any sense of "Here we go again with the same old thing," use a comment like one of the following to affirm those who know the story and to explain the purpose and value of studying this event:

■ "Today we're going to hear one of my favorite Bible stories, and I hope it's one of your favorites, too, because it reminds us of something God never wants us to forget."

■ "I heard this story many times before I really began to see an important truth I needed to learn. I hope that today will help you learn more about this truth, too."

■ "This is one of the best-known stories of all time. But many people who know the facts of the story have never obeyed the teaching of the story."

■ "If you have heard this story before, you may be surprised to find some things the Bible says that you have forgotten."

■ "You may have heard this story when you were younger. But one of the reasons the Bible is such a great book is that as we grow, we can find new truths in places we thought we knew very well."

5. Focus Your Story

If you have ever tried to tell a joke, and then forgotten the punch line, you have a vivid appreciation for the need to have a clear point to every story. No matter how skillfully someone tells a joke, no one will laugh if the punch line is forgotten or garbled. And no matter how skillfully you tell a Bible story, it will have little or no impact unless the point of the story is clear to you and your class.

The stories that Jesus told—and all the stories recorded in Scripture—were intended to cause people to think and then to respond. The whole purpose of the Bible is to be "a lamp to my feet and a light for my path" (Ps. 119:105)—a source of guidance in daily living. No story was placed in Scripture just to provide entertainment. The stories should always lead us to consider our own lives in light of the good or bad example we have studied, and then act on that consideration.

Unfortunately, some teachers get so involved in filling their stories with interesting tidbits and descriptions, that when they come to the conclusion, no one is too sure of what the story is all about. Most first and second graders, and many older children as well, cannot recognize the point of a story on their own. When asked to tell what the story of the Good Samaritan is all about, children's answers will range from, "It's about robbers!" to "It tells about a man and his donkey." Even those who recognize that it's a story about kindness are not likely to conclude that it's a story that teaches us to be kind to anyone who has a need, even if it's someone we dislike.

The teacher must make the point of the story very clear to the children, and to make sure the point does not get lost, the teacher must tell the story so that the point is the focus of all that happens. If more than one main point is illustrated by a story, it is best to select one and emphasize it. One good idea, clearly communicated, is better than several good ideas that no one remembers.

As a general rule, the longer the story becomes, the harder it is to keep it focused. Therefore, keep your story brief. Most of the stories Jesus told can be read in less than a minute. A good rule of thumb for a beginning teacher is to limit your story to one minute for each year of the children's age. Thus, keep a story for six-year-olds to within six minutes. Eleven minutes is a good length for eleven-year-olds. If you have more than one age level in your class, target for the middle of the group, but be ready to shorten the story if the younger ones become listless. While an experienced storyteller may be able to stretch children's attention beyond these limits, it is always better to quit talking before the child quits listening.

Two objections are sometimes raised about this advice to keep a story brief:

■ Some people unthinkingly gauge the value of their story by its length: the longer the story, the more "meat" it's supposed to have. A teacher who tells long stories needs to ask: Am I simply enamored with hearing myself talk? Are my longer stories robbing children of sufficient time for activities to help them remember and apply what the story taught?

■ Some people worry that with a short story, they will not be able to keep the children occupied for the entire session. These teachers need to examine their use of Bible Learning Activities (see chapter 11), as means of reinforcement and application.

6. Plan Your Story Sequence

Every story has five essential ingredients, each of which is needed in order for the story to make sense to children and enable them to remember what they have heard. A good storyteller keeps these five parts of the story clearly in mind, both in preparation and in presentation:

■ *Setting*—Where did the story take place?

In most stories this is the least important of the five factors. However, in Bible stories, stressing the setting helps children recognize that this event happened in the real world, not in never never land or once upon a time.

■ *Character*—who is the main person in the story?

If the main character has an unfamiliar name or occupation, take a moment to introduce him or her before starting the story. Show a picture or flannelgraph figure as you say, "This is a picture of (name), the person this story is about." Present enough details about this person to help your audience care about what happens to him or her.

■ *Beginning Event/Problem*—What happened to the main person?

Something has to happen to set the main character in action and to get the listeners interested in what he or she is going to do. Many of the stories about Jesus begin with someone coming to Jesus with a question or a need. In some stories, the beginning event is an inner feeling, such as David's discontent that led to his sin with Bathsheba. In other situations, the event may not immediately touch the main character, but he or she must soon enter the picture in response to this event.

The problem should always be expressed in terms that make it as relevant as possible to the audience. For example, children may have a hard time empathizing with the social stigma of Sarah's barrenness, but they can easily identify with her loneliness.

■ *Action*—What does the main person do in response to the beginning event?

If the audience is interested in what happens to the main character, they automatically want to know what he or she is going to do in the situation you have presented. Even if they already know the plot, they want to hear at least a summary of the person's quest to resolve the problem.

■ *Result*—What happened as a result of the main character's action?

In many stories, the result of the character's first action is awareness of a new problem which requires more effort from the person. For example, the story of David and Goliath begins with Jesse sending young David to get news of his brothers in the army. The result of that effort was that David heard the challenge of Goliath, which led David to inquire about someone to meet the challenge. The result of David's inquiries was that he decided to meet the giant. This decision led to a meeting with Saul, which finally led to meeting and defeating Goliath. The audience stays with the cycle of events, actions and results because of an interest in that main character's responses in each circumstance.

If you are teaching younger elementary children, present the five parts of the story in their chronological sequence, and limit the story to two or three cycles of events, actions and results. Any variation from that pattern is likely to result in confusion in children's minds and that will reduce their ability to remember what the story is about.

If you teach older children, you may occasionally want to vary the sequence of the story parts and have several more cycles of events, actions and results. The most common storytelling device to vary story sequence is the "flashback." The flashback begins telling the middle or end of the story to arouse interest, then jumps back to the beginning to lead the audience to see what led up to that event. In many cases, the flashback leaves the main character at a moment of decision or peril, leaving the audience in suspense until the narrative catches up to that point. This is a very effective device for breathing "new life" into a very familiar story.

7. Use Your Skills in Communicating

Once you have planned your story presentation, there are some basic guidelines that can help make your presentation most effective.

The first rule is to be yourself. Some people think they must compete with TV cartoons and video games, telling their stories with great dramatic flair. It really is unnecessary that you become a skilled actor, or that you imitate the style of a storyteller you have heard. In dealing with Bible stories, children need the touch of a real person more than they need to be entertained. They need to hear, not only what happened in the story, but what that truth means in real life.

The second rule is to be willing to stretch yourself a little, every time you tell a story. Being yourself does not mean you settle for whatever is easiest for you to do. If you expect your learners to grow as they listen, you need to be growing as you speak. Make a conscious effort to try something new, even if it's uncomfortable for you at first. Every new skill feels awkward the first few times you try it, but with practice, it will gradually become part of your unique style of talking.

Try something new with your *voice:*

■ Try talking a little slower—or faster—to make parts of the story more dramatic.

■ When the suspense builds, talk softer. A whisper is the most dramatic sound the human voice can make.

■ On rare occasions, talk louder—and be considerate of other classes when you do so.

■ Above all, avoid talking down to the children. Talk to them as you would to your best friend. Just watch out that you use words your listeners understand.

Try something new with your *face:*
■ Make a conscious effort to smile as you talk, especially if you have a tendency to be very intense,
■ Occasionally, try matching your expression to the emotion of a character in the story.
■ Work at maintaining eye contact with your children throughout the story. Know your story well enough that you can glance at your notes and then look up. Eye contact can help each child feel you are talking directly to him or her.

Try something new with *gestures:*
■ Avoid nervous habits, such as scratching your head, rubbing your nose, fiddling with a tie or necklace, etc.
■ Fold your hands in your lap or on your Bible until you need them to emphasize something.
■ When you really want attention, use your hands to invite the class to lean in closer to hear what you are saying.
■ Occasionally touch a child's shoulder or hand to convey your interest and concern.
■ Move closer to a child whose attention is wandering.

Try something new with *visuals:*
■ Hold teaching pictures in front of you so that you can show them when you want to and then put them down when you want attention returned to you.
■ Try mounting flannelgraph figures on craft sticks and using them as puppets.
■ Invite children who already know the story to place figures as you talk.
■ Show frames from a Bible story filmstrip as you tell the story.
■ Ask children to tell what they think happened just before or just after the scene in a teaching picture.

Try something new with your *presentation*:
- Use puppets to tell or act out the story. Involve children in using the puppets.
- Lead the class in acting out the story.
  - Provide props and costumes.
  - Have the actors pose scenes for you to photograph.
  - Lead the group in writing captions for each photo.
  - Film or videotape the performance, then view the finished production.
- Invite a guest to portray the main character. Have children primed to ask the guest questions about the story.

8. Involve Your Group in Discovery

The purpose of telling Bible stories to children is to lead them to understand and apply Bible truth. Therefore, the teacher must do more than simply work on developing storytelling skills. Two significant ways in which the teacher can lead a class beyond mere listening is by guiding them in developing Bible skills and by asking questions.

One serious hallmark of the past two decades has been a continuing decline in children's reading ability and in the amount and quality of reading they do. Television absorbs so much of the average child's day that once-common reading skills are threatened. This must concern a Bible teacher, for children need to learn to use the Bible themselves, and not just listen to someone else talk about it.

Thus, a good storyteller also includes opportunity for children to use their Bibles either before, during or after the story presentation:
- Even first graders can be led to *locate* the passage where the story is found. This experience not only gives the child the sense that the story really is from the Bible and not from the teacher's imagination, it also begins to build confidence in learning to handle the Bible. Children can quickly locate most books from which their stories are drawn, either by using the contents page, or by learning to section off their Bible:

• The midpoint of most Bibles is in or near Psalms.

• The midpoint of the first half of the Bible is in or near 1 Samuel.

• The midpoint of the second half is in or near Matthew.

■ After locating a passage, even beginning readers need to be able to *read* for themselves something the Bible says. Rather than just asking a child to read a verse, ask the child to find some specific piece of information in the verse: a person's name, a word, a phrase, a statement, an answer to a question. Often the child who claims to already know the story will be surprised with something he or she read in the Bible. Who doesn't know the story of Daniel in the lion's den? But does everyone know what the king did during the night Daniel was with the lions, or what he shouted into the lion's den the first thing the next morning?

■ Even when a child can read, much patient guidance is needed to help the child learn to *understand* what he has read. Not until third or fourth grade do many children begin to read for "sense." Often a child will read a verse without giving a thought to what it means.

• A specific assignment will start the child on the road to reading the Bible with the intention of understanding.

• Often a following question or two is necessary to push the child into really thinking about the meaning.

• One of the best ways of checking on a child's understanding is to ask, "Can you think of another way to say that?" Or ask, "How would you explain that verse to a friend?"

Along with helping children develop their ability to use the Bible, the storyteller also needs to develop skill in asking good questions. Someone once observed that most questions asked by Sunday School teachers could be answered by one of four words: God, Jesus, Yes or No. A serious indictment! Any child who learned those answers could move from class to class with little or no difficulty. However, if you want your story to capture the imaginations and hearts of your children, you need to ask questions that stimulate them to think.

The most basic type of question is one that asks for informa-

tion or facts. These might be used at the beginning of a story to see how much the group already knows. Or they might be asked at the conclusion of a story as a quick review and to see if everyone was awake during the story. These questions have value in getting children to restate important points, but they tend to sound to a child like a test at school — not a very pleasant association for most children.

The next type of question asks for evidence of **comprehension** or understanding. Try asking children to rephrase an answer or add something to what another child said. Ask questions that ask the child to give a reason (Why?) or to evaluate a story character's actions. One teacher was astonished when his first and second grade class responded unanimously that God was more pleased with the Pharisee's prayer than that of the publican (see Luke 18:9-14). Unless this teacher had asked a question at the end of the story, he never would have realized that his class had missed the whole point of the story and were impressed by the Pharisees boasting and repelled by the sins of the publican.

The third type of question focuses on **application.** Children need to be asked what the story is telling them they should do. Sometimes it is helpful to phrase the question in general terms first: "What is one way a child your age could do what this story teaches?" Sometimes children need to recognize ways in which they have already begun to grow in a certain area: "When have you ever done something (kind, honest, worshipful, etc.) like the person in our story?" But sooner or later the child needs to respond to the question, "What can you do this week to show you want to do what this story teaches?"

Unfortunately, many teachers spend so much time telling the story and then reviewing the facts, they have no time left to lead the children in serious consideration of how to apply its lessons to life. No wonder many older children become bored with "the same old Bible stories." However, the teacher who leads children in answering application questions will see their interest grow as the Holy Spirit uses new and old stories to push them on to new growth in their Christian lives.

RESOURCES FOR TEACHERS AND LEADERS

Axline, Virginia. *Dibs: In Search of Self.* New York: Ballantine, 1976.

Blackwell, Muriel. *Called to Teach Children.* Nashville: Broadman Press, 1983.

Bolton, Barbara. *How to Do Bible Learning Activities: Grades 1-6, Book 1.* Ventura, CA: Gospel Light, 1982.

————*How to Do Bible Learning Activities: Grades 1-6, Book 2.* Ventura, CA: Gospel Light, 1984.

Brown, Lowell. *Sunday School Standards, Revised Edition.* Ventura, CA: Gospel Light, 1986.

————*Teacher Training Manual, Revised Edition.* Ventura, CA: Gospel Light, 1987.

Buchanan, Neal C. & Eugene Chamberlain. *Helping Children of Divorce.* Nashville: Broadman Press, 1982.

Campbell, Ross. *How to Really Love Your Child.* Wheaton, IL: Scripture Press, 1982.

Elkind, David. *A Sympathetic Understanding of the Child: Birth to Sixteen.* Boston: Allyn and Bacon, 1974, 1978.

Mears, Henrietta C. *What the Bible Is All About: Revised Edition.* Ventura, CA: Gospel Light, 1982.

Soderholm, Marjorie. *Explaining Salvation to Children: 8th Edition.* Minneapolis: Free Church, 1979.

Williams, Joyce W., and Marjorie Stith. *Middle Childhood: Behavior and Development: 2nd Edition.* New York: Macmillan, 1980.

Resources for Children

Bible Games for Children. Ventura, CA: Gospel Light, 1981.

Bible Maps for Children. Ventura, CA: Gospel Light, 1981.

Bible Pictures for Children. Ventura, CA: Gospel Light, 19??.

Blankenbaker, Frances. *What the Bible Is All About for Young Explorers.* Ventura, CA: Gospel Light, 1986.

McElrath, William N. *Bible Dictionary for Young Readers.* Nashville: Broadman, 1965.

Sing Praises. Ventura, CA: Gospel Light, 1979.

Sing to the Lord. Ventura, CA: Gospel Light, 1976.

How to Use Bible Learning Activities

"Where do they get all that energy?"
"How will I ever get them to sit still?"
"Do they ever stop moving?"

These are a few of the questions new teachers ask when they first observe a class of elementary-aged children. The level of activity in a group of youngsters is so different from that of a group of adults that the new teacher immediately wonders, "How can I get them to start acting like grown-ups?" The assumption that is made is that learning will only take place when the children are sedately seated, listening to every word the teacher utters—just like all the adults do in their own classes.

Unfortunately, this view does not take into account either the nature of children nor the essence of Bible learning. Consider first that while children may learn by sitting and listening, they learn best when they are actively involved. Children learn by doing! Long after they forget what someone said, they will remember what they did, for actions do speak louder than words!

Second, while it is important for people to hear God's Word, the Scriptures are filled with warnings against focusing on only that one dimension of learning:

"My people come to you, as they usually do, and sit before you to listen to your words, but they do not put them into practice. With their mouths they express devotion, but their hearts are greedy for unjust gain" (Ezek. 33:31).

"Therefore everyone who hears these words of mine and puts them into practice is like a wise man who built his house on the rock. The rain came down, the streams rose, and the winds blew and beat against that house; yet it did not fall, because it had its foundation on the rock. But everyone who hears these words of mine and does not put them into practice is like a foolish man who built his house on sand. The rain came down, the streams rose, and the winds blew against that house, and it fell with a great crash" (Matt. 7:24-27).

"For it is not those who hear the law who are righteous in God's sight, but it is those who obey the law who will be declared righteous" (Rom. 2:13).

"Do not merely listen to the word, and so deceive yourselves. Do what it says" (Jas. 1:22).

Teachers of God's Word have a great responsibility to not merely lead children to listen. Teaching must give them opportunity to put into practice what they have heard. It is not sufficient to merely urge children to go home and do what they were told. Teachers must use a variety of ways by which children can express the truth of God's Word. The vehicles by which this can be done are Bible Learning Activities.

BIBLE LEARNING ACTIVITIES: WHAT ARE THEY?

Bible Learning Activities is the title for one of the three major time blocks in the session (see chapter 11). Each week, children are led to participate in an activity that has been chosen to do more than just fill in the time or to keep the kids busy.

What qualifies an activity for use at Sunday School? How can we be certain that the activity will result in Bible learning? When does an activity become a Bible Learning Activity?

Three important questions must be answered yes before you know if the activity is ready to use with children:

Question 1: Does it teach, review or reinforce a Bible truth?

Question 2: Does the Bible Learning Activity encourage

biblically-oriented research using the Bible itself, and perhaps other tools such as pictures, filmstrips, maps, books, cassette tapes, interviews, field trips, etc.?

Question 3: Will the activity provide opportunity for the learner to relate the Bible truth to everyday experiences? It's the teacher's responsibility to help the child plan for specific ways to make the Bible truth a part of day-to-day actions. The teacher also needs to follow up, to be aware of what happened when the learner attempted to put the Bible truth into practice. This kind of follow-up provides a basis for teacher-student evaluation. It also permits the teacher to be supportive and encouraging as the learner moves toward changing his behavior, a true test of learning.

The plan for each Bible Learning Activity must be specific enough to permit the child to feel assured (as the activity develops) that the activity has purpose and structure. However, it must be flexible enough to take into account the ability and skill level of each learner.

For example, as a teacher prepares for a Bible Learning Activity in which puppets will be used to dramatize a Bible story, that teacher will make sure the activity includes both academic and non-academic tasks (writing and reading the scripts as well as making and using the puppets). A teacher will also offer students opportunities to participate in planning. Often a student's ideas help make the activity more effective than if only the teacher's plans and ideas were used. The teacher is then a learner along with the children.

TYPES OF BIBLE LEARNING ACTIVITIES

Variety is not only the spice of life, it is the key to capturing interest and stimulating learning. The best activity will soon become stale if used repeatedly; also the different learning styles of individual children in a class call for varied approaches to reach each one. While the goal of every activity needs to be to promote Bible learning and life application, there is almost no limit to the many different ways in which those goals can be reached. Over a period of time, every child needs the opportunity to be involved in each of the following types of activities:

1. Art
2. Drama
3. Music
4. Oral Communication
5. Creative Writing
6. Service Projects
7. Bible Games
8. Research

1. Art Activities

Bible Learning Activities involving creative art experiences provide an enjoyable and effective way for children to express what they have learned and to plan for ways to put that learning into action. As you use art activities, remember that the learning *process* is more important than the end *product*. As you select and use art experiences, focus the child's attention on the Bible truth depicted, not on the quality of the work.

For example:

• as a child works to portray an incident in the Bible story, the teacher should ask questions to stimulate the child to rethink the narrative: "What happened just (before/after) the scene you are making?"

"Which person in this scene is a good example to follow? Why?"

The teacher should also ask questions to help the child focus on the main truth illustrated in the story:

"What did you learn about (truth) from the story of (person)?"

"What could you do this week that would show (truth) as (person) did?"

• as a child draws or paints or molds a contemporary scene, the teacher should connect this familiar experience to the Bible story or Bible verse:

"What are you doing in this picture that is the same as what (person) did in our story?"

"How would it help the person in your picture if he/she remembered our Bible verse?"

Benefits of Art Activities

Lesson-related art activities can help a child:

- show in a concrete way an abstract concept such as loving, forgiving, worshiping, serving

- think in terms of specifics (clean my room, take out the trash) as he/she applies a Bible verse ("Children, obey your parents")

- discover/show new learnings (for example, illustrating in proper sequence the events of a Bible story)

- put into practice Bible truths (for example, showing love to others by making tray favors for residents in a convalescent home)

- express thoughts that may be difficult to put into words, such as illustrating a scene from a Bible story.

2. Drama Activities

As with art activities, drama (role-plays, skits, puppets, pantomime, etc.) is of value because of the process the child experiences, not because of the quality of the final performance. Bible stories come alive when children act them out, and Bible truth is seen to be effective when incorporated into contemporary situations.

For example:

• a child portraying a Bible character will clearly recall what that person said and did

• a child speaking through a simple puppet may express thoughts and feelings that would not be likely to be spoken otherwise

• planning to act out a situation will push children to think about the application of Bible truth to that circumstance.

Benefits of Drama Activities

■ Dramatic activities provide a unique opportunity to briefly step into another person's shoes, and experience for the moment some of his or her attitudes and feelings.

■ Role-playing and open-ended situations help children relate Bible truths to present-day experiences.

■ Acting out specific examples of loving, sharing, kindness, friendliness, caring and helping gives concrete meaning to these otherwise abstract words.

3. Music Activities

Music is often used with children as merely something to do until all the latecomers arrive, or as a change of pace from the real learning that is going on in the session. Such limited use of music misses the powerful impact music can have on children's understanding, retention and application of Bible truth. While music is always an important ingredient in the Bible Sharing/ Worship segment of each session, it is also a valuable experience for a Bible Learning Activity group to focus on music participation.

For example:

• a Bible Learning Activity group may learn a new song in order to sing it for others in the department, sharing what they have learned about Bible truth through the words of the song

• a group may compare the words of a song with the words of Bible verses to help them understand and recall the words of Scripture

• a group may combine art and music by illustrating the words and meaning of a song

• children can identify times during the coming week when it would be helpful for them to remember a song they have learned to sing, or have illustrated, or have accompanied with instruments.

Benefits of Music Activities

A Bible Learning Activity involving music is an enjoyable way for children to be actively involved in learning and remembering scriptural truths. Music carefully selected for a specific purpose can help a child:

- learn Bible truths or doctrine
- memorize Scripture verses
- suggest and reinforce Christian conduct
- create an atmosphere of quietness and worship
- move smoothly from one activity to another
- enjoy relaxation and activity.

4. Oral Communication

Talking is a part of all other types of activities, but it can also be the major ingredient in a variety of interesting and valuable activities (brainstorming, interviewing, case studies, Bible reading, etc.). Children respond well to activities that encourage them to express their thoughts and feelings. Since the focus of oral activities is on what the child says, the teacher must give prime attention to phrasing appropriate questions and then listening with sensitivity and understanding.

For example:

• children enjoy formulating questions to use in an interview of a Bible character, a church leader, an adult with specialized knowledge, a missionary guest, etc.

• involving children in retelling the Bible story increases retention and gives children the opportunity to put in their own words the main truth the story conveys

• discussing ways of putting a Bible truth into practice can involve every child in the group in offering ideas and evaluations of the practical implications of God's Word.

Benefits of Oral Communication Activities

Oral communication activities allow children to:

- share their needs, interests, concerns, understanding (and misunderstandings), and possible solutions to problems
- be heard by someone who will listen actively and atten-

tively to what he or she is saying. (Children are often with people who only hear their words, but do not listen with understanding to what a child is saying.);

■ increase their listening skills
■ improve their Bible memory skills.

5. Creative Writing

Creative writing activities can provide valuable learning experiences for children when the experiences are planned according to the abilities of the child and when they hold no threat of failure. Committing thoughts to paper—as a poem, a story, a diary, a stanza to a hymn, etc.—aids a child in recalling and then developing the key thoughts expressed.
For example:

• a beginning reader may dictate words or sentences for the teacher to write, enabling the child to have a visible reminder of ideas expressed in class

• a child who writes a letter to a friend explaining the main point of the lesson is developing skill in sharing the faith with others

• a child who rewrites a Bible verse into his or her own words is having to grapple with meaning, not just rote memory

• a child who contributes a word or phrase to a group composition is encouraged to feel a part of the class and enjoys the success of having his or her ideas accepted.

Benefits of Creative Writing Activities

Lesson-related creative writing activities can help children:

■ list/describe specific, concrete examples of an abstract concept such as loving, forgiving, worshiping, serving

■ express their feelings about God, or about their experiences and needs

■ share Bible information they have discovered

■ crystallize their thinking as they put their ideas into words

■ record ways they put Bible truths into practice in daily life

■ show love to others (for example, writing letters to missionaries or people who are homebound; writing thank-you notes to parents or the church staff; making "I will help you" coupons in which they offer to run errands, etc.)

■ improve their recall of Bible events by organizing and writing information about the Bible story.

6. Service Projects

Service projects allow a teacher to take a class beyond simply hearing about obeying God, talking about obeying God and even planning ways of obeying God. Acts of service done as part of a group are effective ways to help children begin actually obeying God by assisting others.

For example:

• a class may do an art, drama or music activity in order to benefit another class or group

• children may work together to care for church facilities (pick up litter, pull weeds, clean closets, etc.)

• children may invite a non-churched friend to a church activity

• children may adopt a "grandparent" in a rest home, or a missionary child their same age, or child in a children's hospital.

Benefits of Service Project Activities

Service projects that grow out of Bible lessons can help children:

• encourage one another to do what God's Word teaches
• experience the joy of giving to benefit others
• accept responsibility to complete a task
• learn to work together
• recognize that God's Word leads His people to action.

7. Bible Games

Play and learn! Often children are not aware of the direct learning value of a game, but they participate enthusiastically because they enjoy the game. Bible games are helpful tools for involving children in an enjoyable way to discover, use and remember Bible truths and verses.

For example:

• matching Bible words with their definitions can give the teacher opportunity to ask children to tell of times they do or do not show the quality of the word they defined

• playing "20 Questions" about Bible characters can lead children to think of varied actions or qualities of each character

• Bible verses puzzles give repeated opportunities to review the meaning and application of the verses.

Benefits of Bible Games

Through Bible games the child can:

- discover new information
- review Bible truths
- develop skill in using the Bible and research materials
- reinforce skills through practice
- build understandings
- apply Bible truths
- memorize Bible verses
- increase his or her skill in interacting in a group situation (taking turns, being fair and honest).

8. Research Activities

Like oral communication activities, research is a part of every other type of activity, but it can also be an activity on its own. Research is used in Art, Music, Drama, etc., to make sure children are learning accurate biblical information. This may be as simple as looking up a Bible verse, examining a picture or checking a map. Or, research may involve watching a filmstrip, listening to a tape, using a concordance or dictionary. As with the other types of activities, the information is not an end in itself, but is a means to equip the child to put truth into action.

For example:

• a visit to the pastor's office can help clarify the varied roles a pastor fills, and the ways in which pastors help everyone in the church grow as Christians

• working in pairs or trios to locate Bible verses can motivate children to build their Bible use skills, while providing opportunity to review the points expressed in those verses

• watching a film, filmstrip or video related to the lesson will be enhanced by assigning children specific information to garner and report.

Benefits of Research Activities

Research activities help children:

■ develop skill in using their Bibles to locate information

■ develop skill in using Bible study resources such as maps, atlases, concordances, Bible dictionaries

■ discover the meanings of new words and phrases

■ gather information they need about a particular topic

■ explore feelings (for example, discussing the feelings of people in a film can lead them to share/discuss their own feelings about a topic or question).

BIBLE LEARNING ACTIVITIES: HOW TO SELECT THEM

As you consider using Bible Learning Activities in your teaching situation, perhaps you are wondering: How do I know which specific activities to plan?

To answer this question, think first about your goals for the children in your class. Ask yourself, "What experiences will help my children accomplish the aims of the lessons I am teaching?" Consider both the content of the Bible story as well as the desired life application. Make sure that over a period of time you provide a balance of content-centered activities and application-centered activities. Of course, many activities will involve both content review and life application.

Besides the lesson aims, consider these factors in planning the activities for your group:

1. What supplies are available to work with?

2. What kinds of activities have I not provided recently?

3. How much time is available in which to complete the activity?

4. Can the activity extend over a unit of lessons, or will it need to be completed within a single session? Unit-long activities enable you to provide more challenging activities for your group, but a high degree of absenteeism can make it difficult to bring a unit-long activity to completion.

BIBLE LEARNING ACTIVITIES: HOW TO GUIDE THEM

A child is usually motivated to do an activity because of interest in the activity itself. It is the teacher's responsibility to make sure the activity results in real Bible learning, not just activity for activity's sake. Five main steps are needed to accomplish learning effectively in an activity:

1. Introduce the purpose of each activity

When an activity is first presented to children, it is important to explain *why* the children will be doing it, and not simply *what* they will do. Children may choose an art activity because they like to draw cartoons. They need to hear a concise explanation of the reason for those cartoons: e.g., "to help us learn ways to trust God in hard times."

2. Involve children in research

While research may occasionally be an activity all by itself, all other types of activities need to begin with having the children gather some specific Bible information. The method for securing the information must be compatible with children's ability and interests. For example, a first grader may simply read Bible words the teacher has lettered on a chalkboard while a fifth grader will locate and read the verses in the Bible. The older child might use a Bible dictionary to look up any word he does not understand, while the younger child may listen to a taped explanation.

Consider the following research methods for the Bible learning activity you plan. Take into account children's skills and interests.

Audiovisuals

a. *Filmstrips* • Bible stories and material that relate Bible truth to a child's experience are available on a variety of filmstrips with tapes or records. Check your Christian bookstores or curriculum catalog for listings. Your public library may also have similar material. Preview all material before using it with children!

b. *Blank Cassette Tapes* • Cassette players and blank tapes are widely used because they are small, easy to operate, relatively inexpensive and offer many opportunities for use by both children and teachers. A tape recorder becomes an extra teacher when a teacher records information and guidance for children to use in listening and learning independently.

c. *Records/Tapes* • Listening to records or tapes at a listening center with headsets can be an effective means of research. For example, a tape or record can help children understand the words of hymns used in worship. Listening to a story or Bible reading is a good way for children to acquire information.

d. *Video/Motion Pictures* • An increasing number of video and/or motion pictures are available for children's research. Audiovisual suppliers rent a wide range of programs at nominal charges; many public libraries make suitable copies available at no cost. Teachers should preview each program before class use, since not all are appropriate or biblically accurate.

Some films include questions for children to think about as they watch. Then these questions are used as a basis for discussion after the film.

Books

A leader who understands the effectiveness of books can help a child use them in research. Select books within the reading ability of the children. Then decide on specific ways to involve the child in using them. For example, on index cards, letter questions pertaining to information found in the book. (For kinds of questions, see "Guided Conversation" later in this chapter.) Place the cards at the places in the book where the answers can be found. The learner reads the question, locates the answer and writes it on the card. Children can secure information from pictures and maps in a similar way.

a. Bible Resource Tools • It is important for children to become acquainted with Bible dictionaries, commentaries and a concordance. Select these research tools in terms of children's skills and interests. (See Resources.)

Children will benefit from making a Bible dictionary for their Bible study class. On a large chart tablet, alphabetically list Bible words that appear in Bible lessons. Children may illustrate the words by drawing appropriate pictures or by cutting them from magazines or books and pasting these pictures beside appropriate words. This activity results in a resource book, which will have significance for children because of their involvement in its production.

b. Bible Reading • Traditionally, Bible reading has been considered too difficult for most children. We have read passages of the Bible to children, but they have done little Bible reading themselves. However, with the availability of current translations and large-print editions, even the first grader, who is just beginning to unlock the communication process called reading, can recognize words in the Bible. As a child's reading skill increases, he can work more independently in Bible reading. Consider these ways to encourage Bible reading:

■ Be sure that your own Bible reading has meaning. Do you read words only? Or do you read ideas and concepts?

■ Help learners to understand the words they are reading. Ask, "What is another way to say that verse?"

■ Use several Bible translations to aid in discovering the meaning of the passages being read.

■ Ask questions for which the answer can be found in a specific verse.

■ Show a series of pictures. Children match each picture with the appropriate verses they read.

■ Learners will enjoy finding a given word in a portion of the Bible. The passage selected must be related to the Bible lesson. For example, mark Genesis 37:1-5 in Bibles. Select words from the passage and write each of those words on a separate word card, one word per card. The child looks in the marked portion of the Bible for the word on his card. In Genesis 37:1-5, encourage the child to find *Jacob, Joseph, father, coat, son and loved.* Children may choose to add some of these Bible words to their Bible dictionaries.

■ Learners at the fourth, fifth and sixth grade levels who read well may record Bible reading at a listening center. Teachers and learners can use these recordings when visiting absentee students or as an aid to others with reading problems.

■ During the week phone or write to a student, asking him to be ready to read a certain portion of the Bible on the following Sunday morning. Assist him or her with any difficult words. Avoid embarrassing any child by asking him or her to read aloud without a chance for preparation.

■ Choral reading of Bible passages is an excellent way to clarify and reinforce the meaning of the passage. Do not be concerned with exact rhythm, voice quality, or drama details. Reading as a group also gives children who lack reading skills an opportunity to participate successfully in a word-oriented activity.

c. Look and Listen Teams • Two learners may decide to work together to research information about a given subject. This research technique helps children put into practice the concept of acceptance of one another and of working together with a common goal. It will be important for the team members to agree upon the information they need, the materials to be used and ways of reporting to a larger group.

3. Guide the conversation to emphasize the purpose of the activity

Another step in planning effective Bible Learning Activities pertains to the conversation that accompanies them. As children work on an activity, the teacher uses informal conversation to guide a child's thoughts, feelings and words toward the lesson's Bible Teaching/Learning Aim.

Focusing a child's thinking toward the lesson's Bible truth is a major purpose of the teacher's conversation. By being alert to ways of relating things from the child's experience to what God's Word says, a teacher helps that child understand Bible truth.

Questions to stimulate children's thinking are an important part of guided conversation. The simplest kind of question requires a student to recall information previously received. The *knowledge kind of question* ("Who was Moses' brother?") does not stimulate discussion because once the question has been answered, little more can be said.

Comprehension questions are designed to help a child interpret the meaning of information. For example, "How do you think Moses felt when God told him to lead the Hebrew people?" Such questions require students to think before they respond. Because comprehension questions do not require "right answers," they encourage discussion rather than limit it. In fact, each student may suggest a different, plausible answer to the question, thus increasing the opportunity for discussion.

Application questions stimulate students to use information in a personal situation. For example, "When have you felt like Moses must have felt when God told him to lead the Hebrew people?" A student's response allows a teacher to know if learning is taking place.

The use of all three types of questions helps a teacher discover what information a child knows (and doesn't know) about a particular topic. Therefore, guided conversation needs to be a dialogue rather than a monologue.

Guiding the conversation also helps a teacher build a good relationship with each child. Each one needs to feel loved by the teacher and that the teacher is interested in the things that interest the child.

As a teacher guides conversation, several kinds of attitudes need to be conveyed towards children. First, by accepting the child's feelings and ideas, the teacher avoids being judgmental. (Remember, accepting and approving are two different things. Accepting means merely recognizing a child's feelings and ideas without blaming or evaluating.)

Guided conversation also gives a teacher opportunities to express praise and encouragement. Each child needs to know teachers recognize honest efforts and the things that are done well.

4. Lead children to identify what they are learning by doing the activity

As children near the completion of an activity, the teacher should ask them to put into words what they have learned about the main truth of the lesson: "What have you learned about God's forgiveness by working on this puppet skit?" When children find such a question difficult to answer, the teacher knows that more learning is needed.

5. Lead children in sharing with others what they learned

One of the most important steps in the learning process is sharing with someone else what was learned. Children need to be encouraged to do this on a regular basis:

■ The teacher should encourage the child to talk about the activity in relation to the main point of the lesson: "If you were to tell a friend about this activity, how would you explain what you've learned about (Jesus and the children)?" Asking the child to think of what to say to someone else about an activity is a helpful way to lead the child to think of the point of a lesson.

■ During Bible Sharing/Worship, ask for volunteers to tell what they have done in their activity group and what that activity has taught them.

■ Children may share their Bible Learning Activities on one Sunday of the unit. Different activity groups may share their activities on different Sundays, or all groups may share on the last Sunday of the unit. This sharing of group projects can be done in a variety of ways:

a. Children can show what they did while the teacher explains it.

b. The teacher can ask questions to lead children in explaining what they learned.

c. A few children can speak on behalf of the rest of their group.

d. Each group member can offer one or two sentences to tell the most important (or interesting) thing they learned.

As this book has shown, much time and effort is involved in doing an effective job of teaching the Bible to children. You may be mopping your brow at this point and commenting about "all the work" this endeavor requires. Yes, there is a great deal involved in a ministry to children. Why? Because a great deal is at stake. How much effort was Jesus willing to expend for the child He took in His arms when He said, "Whoever welcomes one of these little children in my name welcomes me" (Mark 9:37)? How worthwhile would Jesus consider time spent in bringing children to Him? What effort could a person make that would be of greater value than helping a child, a living example of the kingdom of God (see Mark 10:14)?

RESOURCES

For a wide variety of Bible Learning Activity ideas, see:
Barbara Bolton, *How to Do Bible Learning Activities, Grades 1-6: Book 1* (Ventura, CA: Gospel Light Publications, 1982).
Barbara Bolton, *How to Do Bible Learning Activities, Grades 1-6: Book 2* (Ventura, CA: Gospel Light Publications, 1984).

NOTES

NOTES

NOTES